THE MIND OF CHRIST

Reflestions on the Sermon on the Mount

SAINT SHENOUDA PRESS

The Mind of Christ

Reflections on the sermon on the mount

By: Fr Kyrillos Farag

ST SHENOUDA PRESS
SYDNEY, AUSTRALIA
2022

The Mind of Christ: reflections on the sermon on the mount
By: Fr Kyrillos Farag

COPYRIGHT © 2022
St. Shenouda Press

All rights reserved. Except for brief quotations in critical publications or reviews, no part of this book may be reproduced in any manner without prior written permission from the publisher.

ST SHENOUDA PRESS
8419 Putty Rd,
Putty, NSW, 2330
Sydney, Australia

www.stshenoudapress.com

ISBN 13: 978-0-6451395-6-3

All scripture quotations, unless otherwise indicated, are taken from the New King James Version®. Copyright © 1982 by Thomas Nelson, Inc. Used by permission. All rights reserved.

Contents

Introduction

"For all things that I have heard from My Father I have made known to you.– John 15:15

Have you ever thought about what it means when the Bible says, "We have the mind of Christ" (1 Cor. 2:16)? That is an astounding reality! This means that we have the capacity to think about things the way Jesus Christ would think about them.

This book is a collection of sermons by Father Kyrollos in 2020. Each sermon is given a theme, such as how to think, feel and act like Christ. When we have the mind of Christ, we begin to change our thinking. We begin to view people differently and in turn, approach life differently – in a Christ like way.

Think what would happen in our lives if we would respond to our challenges and obstacles with the mind and attitude of Christ. Spiritual fruit would begin to grow and mature in our lives that our lives would bloom with blessings.

Even with the mind of Christ ready for us to access, we are still very flawed people who can lapse back into our old way of thinking and action. Fr Kyrollos explains in this book how from today develop a Christlike mind and attitude. When Christ's mind dominates our minds, then we will be truly in our right minds.

In Jesus' sermon on the mount He gave us a glimpse of how to think and act like Christ in different situations.

Blessed are The Poor in Spirit

"Blessed are the poor in spirit, for theirs is the Kingdom of Heaven"
(Matthew5:3)

When we look back and try to recall what a person was like when they were young; what were their first words as a baby, or when someone leaves this world, we recall their last words. As humans, this is what we think of; the first and the last words of life.

When we think of Jesus' first words, we remember The Sermon on the Mount. It is strong and mighty and the early Christians lived these words. We remember Jesus' final words which are read on Friday Eve of Holy Week from the Gospel of St. John, Chapters 13 to 17, the Paraclete Chapters.

Here, by the grace of God, we will talk about the Lord Jesus' first words when He was on the mountain; with the people listening to Him, He said, "Blessed are the poor in spirit, for theirs is the kingdom of heaven".

Jesus started with the word 'blessed', which means how lucky, how happy and how joyful. The word 'blessed' is repeated many times, just like in Psalm 119 which we pray in the midnight prayer.

Our Lord Jesus chooses the poor in spirit and this is the basic virtue, acceptable to God with humility. Because mankind fell by pride, which was the cause of their disobedience, Jesus put this as the first blessing. Therefore, true humility comes from the source of the Spirit, not boasting but genuinely from the heart.

The person feels that, without God, they are nothing; "I have nothing to stand before You Lord. I depend fully on You Lord and if You leave me or You don't hold my hand continuously, I will be lost".

The practical way for this 'poor in spirit' is saying always to God, "It is according to Your will Lord, not my will". The person who is poor in spirit submits their life entirely to God and God's will is always foremost in their life.

How do you know God's will if you don't hold His words in your heart? Every time we deal with or interact with people, St. Paul tells us we have two things inside us, bodily law and spiritual law.

The bodily law says, "Your dignity, your pride, your way of talking, your prestige and your appearance".

"I HAVE NOTHING TO STAND BEFORE YOU LORD. I DEPEND FULLY ON YOU LORD AND IF YOU LEAVE ME OR YOU DON'T HOLD MY HAND CONTINUOUSLY, I WILL BE LOST"

The spiritual law says," Blessed is the poor in spirit". Learn how to be poor in spirit, learn how to live in true humility from the heart, learn how to live in poverty. Have you ever seen a poor person full of pride? Never. The poor person always feels broken inside, ashamed, has nothing, no clothes, no feet to stand on. We don't want that way, but we want to live a life poor in spirit. To feel that we are nothing, not boasting, but convinced we have no spiritualities, that we are poor in spirit requiring more spirit, needing God more, just like a crying baby for their mother to feed and nurse them.

Every time you feel you are poor in spirit, cry to the Lord with tears and you will be filled with the Spirit. It is the opposite of what St. John said in the Book of Revelation, "Because you say, 'I am rich, have become wealthy, and have need of nothing'" (Revelation 3:17). This is a huge problem these days. But our Lord tells us that the reward for those who are poor in spirit is the Kingdom of Heaven.

I thank the Lord that I lived with and learned from fathers who lived a life poor in spirit. They lived a life of service at the feet of others, turning off their will; they comforted those who were upset and knelt before the proud. They put a stamp on the hearts of people because of what they did. This is the poor in spirit.

Today, our calling is to live poor in spirit, to understand the meaning of the words that the Lord spoke: "Blessed are the poor in spirit, for theirs is the kingdom of heaven".

Our good Lord, our heavenly Lord, we lift our hearts to You Lord. We ask You Lord to grant us a poor heart, the true one so that we resemble Christ and have His image. To You is the Glory and Honour forever, Amen.

Blessed are Those Who Mourn

"Blessed are those who mourn,
for they shall be comforted"
(Matthew 5:4)

"Blessed are those who mourn"; when we hear these words and consider them, the first question which comes to mind is, "My Lord, according to Your thinking and the teaching of the Bible and the Church and the Apostles, do You want us, in Christianity, to be joyful or to be sad?" In this series, we want to draw closer to God's mind and understand how He thinks.

Undoubtedly God's call for us is to be happy, since the Bible is called the Good News. However, God speaks of sadness in different parts of the Bible. For example, in the Gospel of St. Mark, Christ was sad because their hearts were still hardened (Mark 8:17), and when He entered Jerusalem He cried for the sin of humanity. St. Paul says, "That I have great sorrow and continual grief in my heart for my brethren, my countrymen according to the flesh" (Romans 9:2). St. Paul became sad when he saw lost people who did not turn back to Christ.

St. Paul also spoke of another kind of sorrow when he said, "For godly sorrow produces repentance leading to salvation, not to be regretted; but the sorrow of the world produces death" (2 Corinthians 7:10).

So, my brethren, I think it is clear now what kind of sorrow God is pointing us to. Just like the words in the fraction of the mass, "So be sad my soul, for the sins which created all these pains for your Saviour. Reiterate His pains in front of you" (Fraction for the Only Son).

Now you will agree with me that the message of "Blessed are those who mourn", is the second true natural step of blessing. The person who lives poor in spirit focusing on their life and their sins will see their weaknesses and the impurity of heart and all their actions before God. They will see that they had forgotten God and the fear of God and sinned and fell due to sin. But some people still live in their sin, without repentance, drinking sin like water.

Once God works in and calls the person, He knocks on their heart and door, my beloved son, my beloved daughter saying, "You left Me and went very far, return back from that far place which you went". So, the person starts to grieve on their sins, starts to repent and return to God and the sorrow, which is according to God's will. So, Godly sorrow produces repentance which leads to salvation and not regret.

Therefore, Christianity is truly a call for joy, but not the earthly joy, not the happiness according to the world. This is why Jesus said, "I will see you again and your heart will rejoice" (John 16:22).

Every time we suffer for our repentance and for the salvation of others and for the fall of others and for bearing the suffering of pain, for the sake of God's will, we will rejoice more and more.

St. Paul tells us, "If indeed we suffer with Him, that we may also be glorified together. For I consider that the sufferings of this present time are not worthy to be compared with the glory which shall be revealed in us." (Romans 8:17-18). Not to be compared, that the Lord will come and wipe every tear drop, tears for the sorrow of repentance, for the salvation of one of my beloved holy sorrow. So, the Lord will take me in His bosom and hug me and He will say to me, "I will wipe every tear".

> So, the Lord will take me in His bosom and hug me and He will say to me, "I will wipe every tear".

Therefore, the sorrow which the Lord blesses is the weariness for the sake of the Kingdom. For example, working for the service, struggling in your spiritual life, struggling in fasting and prostrations, struggling to reconcile with others and to obey the commandments. The Bible said, "Those who sow in tears shall reap in joy" (Psalm 126:5). The early fathers have this curriculum in their life; they say, "If we are sinners then with sorrow we will be disciplined and if we are holy then with sorrow we will be tested". Sorrow tests the person. Jesus tasted sorrow on the cross and tasted pain. He said, "My soul is exceedingly sorrowful, even to death" (Matthew 26:38).

This is the sorrow which the Lord was referring to when He said, "Blessed are those who mourn, for they shall be comforted". Therefore, we should not feel angry in sadness, because we will receive true comfort, as the Psalmist said, "In the multitude of my anxieties within me, your comforts delight my soul" (Psalm 94:19).

Today, God calls us to meditate on our life, particularly on our sins, which cause Christ to be sorrowful. It is a call for our repentance. God knocks on my door and your door saying, "My daughter, my son, you went so far away from Me, come back. And when you examine yourself and look for the sins and the sorrow you caused, God will rejoice over you with the joy of repentance.

Our heavenly, good, kind father, today grant us to feel sorrow for our sins and the fall of our loved ones, so we can experience the great joy and establish the complete joy for repentance. To You is the glory and honour, forever Amen.

Blessed are The Meek

"Blessed are the meek, for they shall inherit the earth"
(Matthew 5:5)

We continue to seek to understand the mind of Christ with the third blessing. Jesus said, "Blessed are the meek, for they shall inherit the earth".

Let us ask 'what is meek'? First, let us imagine what a meek person looks like; when they engage in dialogue with others, when they become hurt or provoked. What do they look like then, or how do they react or how patient are they with others? We seek to explain the meek person.

How we are all in need of meekness during these times; as fathers, mothers, servants, the community; therefore, the rest of the verse says, "they shall inherit the earth".

We are able to win others with meekness and gentleness. There is only one thing Jesus asks us to learn from Him, and that is meekness, "Learn from Me, for I am gentle and lowly in heart" (Matthew 11:29).

Meekness and humility are two sides of one coin. You cannot find a meek person who is not lowly in heart and vice versa. Remember my friend, the only thing that the Lord has asked us to learn from Him is meekness. It is true love. The meek person is full of love because "love suffers long and is kind" (1 Corinthians 13:4). When your love is diminished or the storage is low, you find your tolerance for others is also low and there is no meekness. At times, you cannot even tolerate yourself.

We live in a society which is violent; a language different to ours, loud voices. Therefore, as Christians, we should be meek and deal in gentleness with one another. What a shame to not do this. What a pity. As Christians we present a terrible image of Christ and a dreadful image of Christianity. And then we say that Christianity is weak in the world. Yes, because of us.

As previously stated, we can't separate meekness from the lowly heart. Every true, meek person is lowly in heart. At times a person may present meekness externally, but their heart is not humble or lowly from within. Hence, as you draw closer to them they can't tolerate you. Also, at times, a person may think their heart is lowly, but as you draw closer to them and perhaps disagree with them, they do not behave as a meek person. Therefore, the meekness is not genuine but false.

Perfect meekness is absolute humility, covered fully in gentleness, peaceful, calm, easy-going and loved by all. Isaiah said, "My Elect One in whom My soul delights! I have put My Spirit upon Him;

He will bring forth justice to the Gentiles. He will not cry out, nor raise His voice, nor cause His voice to be heard in the street. A bruised reed He will not break, and smoking flax He will not quench" (Isaiah 42:1-3). All of these are signs of meekness.

The beautiful picture and icon of meekness is Jesus Christ. Hence, the true Christian has a heart with God and is truly meek in Christ. Isaiah wrote of Christ, "He was oppressed and He was afflicted, Yet He opened not His mouth; He was led as a lamb to the slaughter, and as a sheep before its shearers is silent, So He opened not His mouth" (Isaiah 53:7). But He was praying for all of humanity, interceding for all of us before our heavenly Father.

This is the picture of meekness; the meekness that inherits the earth. How beautiful is meekness? A sweet aroma which reigns on all hearts. This is how the holy saints mastered the virtue of meekness and the gentle voice. Truly this is a rare currency nowadays. St John of the Ladder said, "God finds rest in the meek heart, but the troubled heart is a place for the devil. The meek shall inherit the earth or they will have authority over it."

Meekness is absent from our world and truly a rare currency nowadays. Violence has increased and meekness has decreased. These days the gentle or soft voice and acceptance of others is seen as a weakness. The harsh or loud voice is seen as strength and power. Self-control is almost non-existent. That which is wrong is the norm and the default character trait.

> "GOD FINDS REST IN THE MEEK HEART, BUT THE TROUBLED HEART IS A PLACE FOR THE DEVIL. THE MEEK SHALL INHERIT THE EARTH OR THEY WILL HAVE AUTHORITY OVER IT."

However, the truly meek Christian will be the salt over all the earth and have the true love. We are called to be meek. True meekness is the fruit of a relationship with God and the work of the Holy Spirit in us. It is not our work or personal effort, but rather it is the meekness that inherits the earth and wins souls.

This is our call today, our heavenly, kind Father. Give us a true relationship with You. Let us grow in every good deed and be meek, so that we will win the temporary earthly and the eternal heavenly. To You is the glory and honour forever and ever. Amen.

Blessed are Those Who Hunger and Thirst

"Blessed are those who hunger and thirst for righteousness, for they shall be filled" (Matthew 5:6)

Each of us considers and cares for their own flesh; our need to eat and drink and so on. But do we give the same attention to our spiritual food and drink? When we neglect the food for the soul, it becomes weak and does not influence the body. Then, the body takes control and the person becomes bodily.

The words, "blessed are those who hunger and thirst for righteousness", are a wonderful promise from God to all those who strive for this hunger for righteousness, for God promised that, "they shall be filled".

I will tell you a true story which happened to a very close friend of mine. During a certain time in his life he worked in a place where there was no church. The closest church to him was a 2 hours plane trip and this was not convenient to do. So, he was there in this place with no church, no Holy Communion and no Bible. He was hungry for God and thirsty for God's righteousness. One day he prayed earnestly from the Psalms, "Early I will seek You, my soul thirsts for You" (Psalm 63:1). He continued in prayer for many hours. He went deep in his prayers and cried to God saying, "Lord, I am thirsty, I am hungry, I am eager to see You, to eat You, to touch You". As he knelt in prayer, suddenly the room was filled with a bright, white light and he saw the Lord Jesus standing in front of him with His wounds. I am sharing this story with you so that you know that God is always calling us to enjoy Him and spend time with Him and He asks us to be hungry and thirsty for Him.

God is faithful to anyone who needs Him. It was said by one of the early church fathers, "This is the job of anyone who pleads to God with tears". David said in Psalm 42:1-3, 5, "As the deer pants for the water brooks, so pants my soul for You, O God. My soul thirsts for God, for the living God. When shall I come and appear before God? My tears have been my food day and night, while they continually say to me, 'Where is your God?' Why are you cast down, O my soul? And why are you disquieted within me? Hope in God, for I shall yet praise Him for the help of His countenance".

How beautiful is the person who thirsts for God? God promised that they will be filled. Let us come to Him now.

What is righteousness that the Lord talks about it in this blessing? It is the righteousness of God in Christ, for we have no righteousness without Christ. Outside Christ we have self- righteousness and this takes us backwards as St. Paul said in Romans 3:22, "The righteousness of God, through faith in Jesus Christ, to all and on all who believe".

God's righteousness is a combination of His faithfulness, mercy, love, justice and judgement to mankind. Although we have all sinned and have inherited Adam's sin, but Christ will wipe all of these on His cross and with His blood. In 2 Corinthians 5:21, St. Paul said, "For He made Him who knew no sin to be sin for us, that we might become the righteousness of God in Him". So, there is no righteousness other than the righteousness of Christ.

St. Stephen stood and said in Acts 7:52, "Which of the prophets did your fathers not persecute? And they killed those who foretold the coming of the Just One".

This is the Incarnation of the birth of Christ. It is not something new, but from eternity. God always calls us to come near Him, "You thirsty people, come to the water and those who have no silver come", "Everyone who thirsts, come to the waters; And you who have no money, come, buy and eat. Yes, come, buy wine and milk without money and without price". (Isaiah 55:1).

He calls us, He promises that we will be filled. God's gift, waiting for the person who needs it. One of the fathers said, "This virtue wants you to want it". This means that you want it, you need it. This virtue is expensive, so the hunger and thirst for righteousness leads to being filled and the thirst for righteousness leads to being refreshed. Just as Christ said to the Samaritan woman, "Whoever drinks of this water will thirst again, but whoever drinks of the water that I shall give him will never thirst". (John 4:13-14).

So, we aim and pray for that thought to be within us, to live in us and dwell in us. This is what God wants for us. He says to us, be hunger and thirst for Me, stay with Me and I will fill you and comfort you.

THE HUNGER AND THIRST FOR RIGHTEOUSNESS LEADS TO BEING FILLED AND THE THIRST FOR RIGHTEOUSNESS LEADS TO BEING REFRESHED.

Our good Lord, our holy Lord, grant us today the grace to be hungry and thirst for You, our Holy, Living Water. To always thirst for You, not just once or twice, but we say with David, "My soul thirst for You Lord". To You is the glory and honour forever and ever. Amen.

Blessed are the Merciful

"Blessed are the merciful, for they shall obtain mercy"
(Matthew 5:7)

Mercy is an attribute of God who is merciful. The Book of Exodus tells us that, "The Lord, the Lord God, merciful and gracious, longsuffering, and abounding in goodness and truth" (Exodus 34:6). The Bible talks of God's mercy. The only merciful one is God and every mercy is attributed to our Lord or a reflection of Him. In other words, as we draw closer to God and our hearts become connected to Him, then we live His mercy and practice it with others. This means we become more like God and we imitate Him and adopt His characteristics.

Many asked Him, "Son of David, have mercy on us", like the blind man who called out to Him. This mercy is a free gift, granted by God to those who are merciful; as the verse says, those who are merciful shall obtain mercy. The word of God also says, unless you forgive you will not be forgiven; this mercy is conditional. We will talk about the areas of mercy later. However, in the meantime, know that the more you are merciful with others the more God will show you mercy.

The most important aspect of mercy is forgiveness. God has given us many opportunities to forgive others. The most well-known of Christ's parables explaining an act of mercy is found in Matthew 18:23-35; the Parable of the Unforgiving Servant. There was a king who pardoned one of his servants who owed him 10,000 talents. This was about 6,000 Denarii and equivalent to about $60 million in today's terms. In those days, the daily wage of a labourer was one Denarii. After the king pardoned him, this servant went out and met another servant who owed him just 100 Denarii, a small sum in comparison. This servant could not pay him back what he owed, so the first servant, who had been pardoned by the king, had him thrown into jail until he could pay it all back. Eventually, when the king found out that his servant, whom he had forgiven, did not have mercy on the other servant, said to him, "You wicked servant! I forgave you all that debt because you begged me. Should you not also have had compassion on your fellow servant, just as I had pity on you?" And his master was angry and delivered him to the torturers until he should pay all that was due to him. So, our Lord Jesus concluded by saying, "So My heavenly Father also will do to you if each of you, from his heart, does not forgive his brother his trespasses." (Matthew 18:35).

Therefore, the most important area of mercy is forgiveness, but we think and invent excuses for NOT FORGIVING others. The main reason for not forgiving others is our hardened heart (a heart which has no mercy).

The Church continuously asks God for His mercy (Kirye-layson) and we ask for forgiveness but we do not forgive each other. We also forget that we will be asked by our Heavenly Father why we haven't forgiven others. At the end of the liturgy during the Great Lent, the Church chants "blessed are the merciful on the poor".

The second parable which the Lord Jesus emphasises to enrich our minds and enhance our understanding and hearts on mercy is the Parable of the Good Samaritan (Luke 10:25-37). After telling this parable our Lord asked the lawyer who was listening, which one acted mercifully to the injured man? He answered the Samaritan man who was merciful to him. The Lord told him you go and have mercy on others likewise.

We ask the question, what are the areas of mercy? And who is worthy of mercy?

The following story helps us to understand this. A woman came to the famous French Napoleon Bonaparte and interceded for her son to be forgiven. He replied, "I forgave him the first time but he underestimated my mercy". She replied, "You are a merciful person, please do it again". He said, "No, he does not deserve my mercy". She said, "If you have mercy on a person who deserves it, then it is not counted, but if you have mercy on someone who does not deserve it then it is truly an act of mercy". For some time, he was speechless then he realised that she was right and he pardoned her son completely. This is the true meaning of mercy.

St. Paul said, "For if when we were enemies we were reconciled to God through the death of His Son, much more, having been reconciled, we shall be saved by His life" (Romans 5:10). When we were enemies of God we were reconciled with Him through the death of His Son. Being enemies of God means we are against Him, we turn our backs on Him and resist His will. Thus, we do not deserve His mercy but He is still merciful to us. He has mercy on the poor, the oppressed and the weak.

> "IF YOU HAVE MERCY ON A PERSON WHO DESERVES IT, THEN IT IS NOT COUNTED, BUT IF YOU HAVE MERCY ON SOMEONE WHO DOES NOT DESERVE IT THEN IT IS TRULY AN ACT OF MERCY".

The person who is weak in his anger, abilities, circumstances, up-bringing is the person who deserves mercy. Therefore, we should be merciful to all so that we become deserving of God's mercy.

Our good, gentle Lord, we thank you because you are the merciful God, kind and compassionate. Your mercy is always part of your goodness and gifts to mankind. Give us the will to meditate on this message, to learn and practice mercy towards all people without any discrimination and/or condition according to your grace. To You is the glory and honour forever and ever. Amen.

Blessed are the Pure in Heart

"Blessed are the pure in heart,
for they shall see God"
(Matthew 5:8)

This is the hardest of the blessings. Take care my beloved, there are levels similar to a ladder; the poor in heart, the merciful, those who mourn, until you reach this step, which is the hardest one of all; the pure in heart.

Before we talk about the pure in heart, let us ask one question. What is the heart? We need to go to the early church fathers when we talk about this. According to them, biblically, the heart is the base from which comes all the effects of the spiritual and physical life; "Keep your heart with all diligence, for out of it spring the issues of life" (Proverbs 4:23).

The Bible and the Lord Jesus' teachings give us many kinds of hearts. Christ said, "A good man out of the good treasure of his heart brings forth good; and an evil man out of the evil treasure of his heart brings forth evil. For out of the abundance of the heart his mouth speaks" (Luke 6:45). Hence, there is action in the heart which affects the whole person; good heart and evil heart.

According to the church fathers, the heart is the centre of the whole human being. Therefore, say the fathers, the heart is the centre of ability, energy, intelligence, insight, will, wisdom, vision, emotion, the conscious and all that proceeds from it; just as doctors see how the brain works in the body.

Therefore, when God chooses to meet with a person and dwell in them, He chooses the person's heart, "My son, give me your heart", "You shall love the Lord your God with all your heart, with all your soul, with all your strength, and with all your mind" (Luke 10:27). This is the place which the Lord wants to own and the devil attacks the individual from there. What enters the heart are evil thoughts which one holds on to. The Lord said I cannot dwell with darkness. There is no communion between God and Belial; there is no fellowship between light and darkness. God cannot enter because He wants to own the whole heart. Our God is a jealous God, he wants the whole heart, give Me your heart; until the person realises this point and their spiritual vision opens.

St Makarios the Great said in his homily, "The heart is the castle in which the Lord enters and rests. It is the place which He steers the ship, He orders and manages the life of the person. He is the captain of the person's ship. He holds the rudder to make it go faster or slow it down, to turn it left or right. So, the heart holds the deepest emotions within a person, feelings of tenderness, kindness, mercy. And this is why our Lord chose the heart to dwell in and this is what God wants from us

The pure heart is the most precious gift which God gives to the person who insists on asking for it and who dwells with God. Struggle to obtain this gift and ask for it, like David did, "Create a pure heart in me O God" (Psalm 51:10). God must give this to the person saying, I will give you a new heart and I will take away the heart of stone and give you a heart of flesh; like the new birth which you obtained in baptism and which you protect, through struggles, for your entire life.

Purity of heart is not only that evil does not dwell in my heart, but that the heart be filled with the love of God. This is the pure heart.

When you think deeply, a pure heart means a heart full of God's love, the love of righteousness. To put it simply, a pure heart is filled with the Holy Spirit. This is why Anba Abraam continuously repeated during the night, "Create in me a clean

WHEN YOU THINK DEEPLY, A PURE HEART MEANS A HEART FULL OF GOD'S LOVE, THE LOVE OF RIGHTEOUSNESS.

heart, O God, and renew a steadfast spirit within me" (Psalm 51:10). He understood the meaning of a pure heart and pursued this daily, knowing that a pure heart is the assurance and key to the Kingdom of Heaven.

Many of the early church fathers spoke on the pure heart. Mar Isaac the Syrian, taught how to protect the heart from evil and from the senses. The fathers agreed that the senses are the entrance of a pure heart. The eyes, the tongue, the ears are the doors to protect and preserve not only the senses but also to protect the heart from evil, from holding a grudge, or from hate and lack of forgiveness, which is the huge wall that prevents the purity of heart; this may cause the heart to be closed completely.

Our good Lord, our Holy Lord, our great Lord, who is capable of all things, create a pure heart in me O Lord and renew a steadfast spirit within me. Clean my heart Lord, protect my heart, grant me a good heart, the beautiful heart in which all good things come from. We know Lord that this is beyond our capacity. It is heavenly work not human work. Create this type of heart in us O Lord; "I give you a new heart". To You is the power, the glory and the honour forever and ever. Amen.

Blessed are the Peacemakers

"Blessed are the peacemakers, for they shall be called sons of God" (Matthew 5:9)

There is no doubt that Jesus is the King of Peace. When we consider the birth of Jesus Christ, all the multitude of the heavenly host and angels chanted, "Glory to God in the highest, and on earth peace".

Before Christ left this world, as He ascended to heaven, His farewell words were, "Peace I leave with you, my peace I give to you; not as the world gives do I give to you" (John 14:27). He promised that no one will take our peace from us.

St. Paul said, "For He Himself is our peace" (Ephesians 2:14) and Isaiah said, "Prince of Peace" (Isaiah 9:6). The core of Jesus' service and the depth of His service is peace, to reconcile with us, to make peace with us, between God and man, between heaven and earth and humanity, He is our peace.

The devil always strikes us on this point; fights the person from two sides. The first side is the internal peace. As priests we often hear the comment "I've lost my peace". The other side is to create no peace between you and those around you. The opposite of peace is worry. This is a by-product of the devil. His presence in our life is excessive worry. We worry about everything; he enters the heart and the mind.

The definite sign of God's presence in any place is peace. Every decision you take which has peace, you know is from God. Any prayer you say which is not accompanied by peace, you know is a prayer not prayed well. Most of the things we need in our life are related to peace and the things we want most from others is to be peacemakers and to plant peace between others.

THE DEFINITE SIGN OF GOD'S PRESENCE IN ANY PLACE IS PEACE.

People need peace. Believe me, most people say they don't want anything other than to live in peace. The world needs peace, and as we are sons and daughters of Christ, who is the peacemaker, we should be peacemakers.

The person who plants, builds and spreads peace is a very loving person, from heaven and from earths point of view. From heaven, God says, this person is my son, "be called sons of God", like God, like his creator. And they will be loved on earth because people need peace. Believe me, being a peacemaker is very simple, but requires a very important thing, that the person has a big heart, full of love. Those who have lots of love are peacemakers. They make and plant peace between others, reconcile others together and reconcile them with God.

In spite of all this we often find a lack of peace in communities. Often homes are affected when there is no peace and services are affected when there is no peace. The Gospel of St. John tells us about Satan that, "He was a murderer from the beginning" (John 8:44). He always plants hatred, chaos and weeds between people. The source of peace which we always point to and emphasize on, is God Himself, Jesus Christ. He is the only one who can free our heart from Satan's power. When Jesus owns the heart, He will be the source of peace in our life.

When a person's goal is worldly and materialistic they will lose their peace. The way of Christ is not the way of the world. The two lines will never meet or agree.

How can I be a peacemaker? First, I must point out to the whole world that the source of peace, the way towards peace, can never be without Jesus Christ. As St. Paul says in his epistle to the Romans, "How beautiful are the feet of those who preach the gospel of peace, who bring glad tidings of good things" (Romans 10:15).

Let us look to the example of Abraham and Lot. Abraham refused to have a dispute with Lot. He was a peacemaker, he left everything. Nothing is more precious than peace. If anything comes between you and another person, leave everything for the sake of peace.

Second, we need to avoid gossip. The planting of dispute is deception, "The Lord hates... one who sows discord among brethren" (Proverbs 6: 16,19). Instead of transferring words of discord amongst each other, come and transfer good words, positive words, beneficial words. These do not come from within us but come when we are closer to God.

I'd like to tell you a nice story which I read many years ago when I was young, about someone who planted peace. There was an elderly monk who lived in the wilderness. This monk was respected and honoured by all and many came from far and wide seeking him. After some time, a young monk came and dwelt in the wilderness close to the elderly monk. This young monk was full of virtues and soon all those in the area began to smell his aroma and they came especially to see him and stopped seeking the elder father. One day the elder monk told his disciple to go to the younger monk and tell him to leave this area and go to a different place. His disciple was embarrassed and instead told the younger monk that his teacher thanks you and blesses you and asks you to pray for him. The elder monk asked his disciple if he had passed the message to the younger monk. He repeated the same message to his disciple, instructing him to go and tell the younger monk to leave this area. This time the disciple told the younger monk that my teacher says you are great and asks for your prayers. This disciple planted peace between the elder monk and the younger one.

Finally, the elder monk said, "I will go myself and get him out of this area since until now he is still here". When the younger monk heard that the elder monk was coming, he ran to him and knelt before him; he thanked him for the encouraging messages he had sent through his disciple. The elder monk said, "I thought I was a good teacher, the best, but from now on my disciple will be my teacher and I will be his disciple because he made peace and became like our Teacher Jesus Christ.

Our good Lord, our kind Lord, the gentle one, on this blessed day, grant us grace to resemble Your Son, the King of Peace, the Prince of Peace and to make peace also. To you is the glory and honour forever and ever. Amen.

Blessed are Those Who are Persecuted

Blessed are those who are persecuted for righteousness' sake, for theirs is the kingdom of heaven. (Matthew 5:10)

Since these two blessings are combined, we will discuss them together. Truly, they are very hard to put in practise. Realistically, which one of us can accept to be hit for the sake of the Kingdom, or persecuted, or insulted? This is hard, but let us reconsider; is it truly hard? Or are we seeing a false picture of Christianity?

First, what is justification? We are justified by faith, the cross, the death and the resurrection of Christ. Justification by Christ, our salvation, which we received as a gift. It is not something to be taken lightly. Because we are so immersed in this world, we don't feel for Him or even think of Him, not realising the great gift we have. Think of justification. What is it? To put it simply, consider a person who has committed a serious crime. Should they not be given a severe punishment, according to the law, possibly death? Then someone comes along and takes their place, justifying that person and the outcome changes from death to life. And not just to live, but to live in the highest level of honour. This is the justification that the Lord did for us.

So, because of the devil's envy and jealousy, he aggravates the world against us so that we don't reach this level of honour. The outcome is the world persecutes us and is against us.

The Bible is full of examples. After Jesus healed the blind man in the Gospel of St. John, being justified by our Lord, he was immediately removed from the temple. St. Stephen was persecuted and stoned to death. As soon as the Church began preaching Christ there was persecution and the followers of Christ were dispersed outside Jerusalem.

It is an honour to bear pain and persecution for the sake of Jesus Christ. Those who did that were called the confessors and martyrs. The church has given them a high rank. But you and I are not confessors nor martyrdoms, once our pride is involved we are not anything. We become angry, get steamed up and defend ourselves when anyone says something wrong to us. But our Lord Jesus is completely different. There's a big difference between hearing the words of Christ and applying them in our life. There was a big difference between current times and the times of the Apostolic fathers and how they dealt with persecution.

> IT IS AN HONOUR TO BEAR PAIN AND PERSECUTION FOR THE SAKE OF JESUS CHRIST.

St. John Chrysostom was an excellent homilist, but was persecuted by Empress Eudoxia. Whilst in prison, he wrote to Bishop Kyriakos saying, "When I was taken away from the city, it did not bother me. I said to myself, 'If the Empress wants to isolate me, let her do it. The Lord has the land, He is everywhere. If she wants to saw me in half, I see Isaiah and if she wants me to sink into the ocean, I think of Jonah. If she puts me in the fire, I find the three young men who withstood the fire and if I stand before violent animals, I remember Daniel in the lion's den. If she wants me stoned, I see St. Stephen the first martyr standing before me. If she wants my head, let her have it, I will see St. John the Baptist, shining before me. Naked I came from my mother's womb and naked I shall leave this world'".

St. Paul reminds us, "Do I seek to please men? For if I still pleased men, I would not be a bondservant of Christ" (Galatians 1:10). This is the mature Christian. St. John Chrysostom had a great perspective, he looked towards God, he understood the true message of Christianity.

Consider our fathers the Apostles and what they did in Acts 5. They were in the common prison and the angel of the Lord opened the prison doors and brought them out. They entered the temple again the following morning and continued teaching. They were imprisoned again and again and were threatened with death but, 'blessed are you when they revile and persecute you'. Eventually, Gamaliel instructed that they leave them alone. They had them beaten and they commanded them not to preach in the name of Jesus again and then let them go. It's incredible what our fathers the Apostles did. They should have been fearful but, on the contrary, "They departed from the presence of the council, rejoicing that they were counted worthy to suffer shame for His name" (Acts 5:41).

True love is experienced by pain. It is a fact. It has a price and love suffers for whom it loves. Jesus' stripes were healed. He paid a great price for the pain. The saints took this as a chance to show and express their love for their Saviour and an acknowledgement of His sufferings.

Today, we experience many opportunities for pain and suffering for the sake of Christ, "Blessed are those who are who are reviled and persecuted for my sake".

The question I would like to put forward to you and I today is, how are we doing regarding these things today?

Our Good Lord, our Holy Lord, who suffered pain *for* our sake in order to justify us, grant us Lord to understand our Christianity, truly and to live it the right way and close our mouths and bear the small things *for* the sake *of* what You did and continue to do *for* us. To You is the glory and the honour, *forever* and ever. Amen.

You are the Salt of the Earth

"You are the salt of the earth; but if the salt loses its flavour, how shall it be seasoned? It is then good for nothing but to be thrown out and trampled underfoot by men. (Matthew 5:13)

After our Lord Jesus finished all the Blessings on the mountain, He said the very famous words, "You are the salt of the earth". Here, the Lord divides us into two kinds of salt, good salt and bad salt. Salt is very important in our lives; it dissolves in everything and preserves everything, it gives taste and you can't separate it. You boil it, you freeze it and it remains the same. It retains its chemical structure and never changes. This is our role on this earth. But the question is, "My God, am I the good salt or the bad salt?

The Lord has given us a very important role with a great responsibility. He said, "You are the salt which I will work with in this world. I put you in the midst of people, dissolve in them, live with them and you will protect this world and it will be an excellent world.

The sign of the good salt is it attracts all. The greatest attraction in our Christianity is our love of God. This is our capital. The good salt has love for God. Live with God without being affected by your surroundings. What makes salt lose its saltiness? When you dilute it with lots of water. Likewise, the Christian, when they are dissolved in the world, they lose their saltiness and lose their influence, becoming too flexible. This is happening to many of us.

Look at a mirror and ask yourself what type of salt you are. Am I good salt or bad salt? I'll tell you what this mirror is? Consider your actions, your mind, your behaviour. Are they directed by the Bible or not?

Reflect on the colour of salt. It is white. Consider the purity of your heart, your holiness, your honesty, your dealings with others, your language. Whenever your language and words are good, the words that you speak amongst others, will identify which type of salt you are.

What is your spirit like when you are among people? At work, how you influence others and the words you use. All these things are salt living amongst people.

The good salt is merciful to others, with a good heart, full of kindness, where the source is the love of God. The good salt brings peace to every place, in a troubled world, full of worries and depression.

So, what is our role? Is it to add to the worries or to bring peace to this world? This is the role for you and I in this world. This comes naturally when we are dissolved in Jesus, a living Christ in us who influences others.

Look now inside and outside the house of God, are we influential or are they just words we use? Activities but no true spiritual life from within. No holiness, no purity, no love. I am afraid to say this, and it may cause people to be offended by me, but unfortunately, there is no bond between people, the little atoms of salt have been separated.

> THIS COMES NATURALLY WHEN WE ARE DISSOLVED IN JESUS, A LIVING CHRIST IN US WHO INFLUENCES OTHERS.

This is not God's plan for us. He said you are the salt on earth. We must do our work, we must be the good salt, otherwise, "It is then good for nothing but to be thrown out and trampled underfoot by men".

We need to understand how to live and dissolve in Christ. We must wake up and fulfil our role. If the salt lives for itself, it won't work. Your role is a very important one. You can't say, it is not my role or I can't be salt and it has no relation to wealth or poverty or greatness. All you need to focus on is that you are the salt of the earth.

I know a homeless person, who is going through hardship and tribulation. But nevertheless, he knows his responsibility very well. Although he lives on the streets with no food or clothing, yet his role is to write verses on a piece of paper and when he goes to the coffee machines at the shops he leaves a verse there for someone to find. When he meets people, he talks about Jesus with them. If he has a small amount of money he shares it with others. I was very touched by this young man who understood his role, in spite of all the hardship that he goes through and even though he has the right to blame the entire world for his unfortunate circumstances, yet he lives his life as salt of the earth.

Please hear from me today, when I say you are a Christian, you have to be a salt and to live the life of salt. Your life is important. Who are you? God placed this role on you and I, and it is a huge responsibility. Enough pointing the finger at others, criticising others, hating others, fighting with others, enough. Come, live truly as salt. Let us start from within. Inside the house. Inside yourself. Reconcile with God. Understand your role and live for Jesus.

Our Good Lord, our Holy God, who created us as a salt in this world, grant us grace to understand and to live as the good salt. To You is the glory and honour, forever and ever. Amen.

You are the Light Of the World

"Let your light so shine before men, that they may see your good works and glorify your Father in heaven" (Matthew 5:16)

Christ said of Himself in John 8, "I am the light of the world". Oh God, you gave us the honour to be called light, like You! This is a huge responsibility on each one of us. When Christ said, "No longer do I call you servants ... but I have called you friends" (John 15:15), He is saying we are like Him. However, we are not the source of light, this is the difference. He is, "The true Light which gives light to every man coming into the world" (John 1:9). He lights up the darkness, but we reflect His light, this is the difference, we reflect the light of Jesus Christ.

It is our responsibility and we are assigned to it. Just like being assigned a huge task like St. Paul said, "That you may become blameless and harmless, children of God without fault in the midst of a crooked and perverse generation, among whom you shine as lights in the world" (Philippians 2:15).

When we cover a very strong light, the light won't show. So, it is when we cover God's light in us. God gave us and assigned to us to be a light. So where is the problem? The problem is our selection. We choose to go back to being slaves, we go back to sin. After we start with the spirit, we go back for the flesh, happy to be a slave to the devil, to sin, to impurity. God wants us to be like a lamp stand on the rooftop that gives light to all who are in the house.

So, today the Lord tells us to be a light in our own house first, leave outside. If you want to know if you are a light, look inside your house, your dealings with the members of your family. Sometimes people have a certain image outside but inside they are different. Your mirror is your house: "They may see your good works and glorify your Father in heaven".

Our life should be interpreted as good deeds and good works. St. Paul tells us, "For we are His workmanship, created in Christ Jesus for good works, which God prepared beforehand that we should walk in them" (Ephesians 2:10).

We lost our identity because we stopped doing good works. We are involved in many activities, but not good works. Many activities but the lamp is not lighting the inside of the house. St John Chrysostom said, "The light is the Holy Spirit", which is inside you and I. God gave us the Holy Spirit to give light to us and what are we doing? We extinguish the light inside us when we cover the light. He told us to live the right way and do good works.

I will tell you this story: A young man worked for a well-known company. One of his colleagues, a young Asian man, was notably successful with this organisation. The young man noticed that his colleague disappeared every lunch time. One day he asked him where he had been? His colleague replied, "I go to the meeting room nearby, close the door and pray for each person in our company, that they may know God, draw close to Him and that their hearts may be filled with the love of Christ". The young man asked his colleague if he does this every day. He replied, "Yes, come and join me". The young man asked, "So what is your dream?". His colleague replied, "That everyone in this company know God and their hearts be filled with the Light. Then, I will leave this company and go to another and do the same and so on. I live to pray for others".

Can you see how great it is to be a light and salt for others? To smell this beautiful aroma. So, what should we do, and what is our work? Don't be selfish, living in a cocoon of desires and sin. Be filled with the light, with the word of God, away from darkness, away from the wrong sort of people.

The lamp always needs oil and the oil needs good works and the good works require grace and grace requires the Holy Spirit. So ask, be filled. Every day say to the Lord, "Fill me with Your Holy Spirit". Do everything in the name of the Lord. St. Paul tells us, "And whatever you do, do it heartily, as to the Lord and not to men" (Colossians 3:23). Hence, give the best you have to the Lord, every day. Imagine you have a garden, pick the best of the flowers and hand them to God. It does not matter how small it is, as long as it is the best that you have to give to God. Don't forget your responsibility which you have been assigned to. If you did something wrong, say to yourself, "Is what I have done right? I made the light become dark and put the lamp under a basket".

> THE LAMP ALWAYS NEEDS OIL AND THE OIL NEEDS GOOD WORKS AND THE GOOD WORKS REQUIRE GRACE AND GRACE REQUIRES THE HOLY SPIRIT. SO ASK, BE FILLED.

Our Good Lord, the Light of the world, who allowed us to join in Your light and gave us this huge responsibility, grant us the grace every day to live to be a light for the world. To You is the glory and honour forever and ever. Amen.

The Lord Fulfils the Law

"Do not think that I came to destroy the Law or the Prophets. I did not come to destroy but to fulfill. (Matthew 5:17)

The Lord begins here by stating that He did not come to destroy but to fulfil the Law which Moses received on the two tablets that were written by the finger of God, the Ten Commandments. Jesus said, I did not come to destroy but to fulfil, I am coming to continue the Law, I am the founder of the statute of perfection and the Author of the Law, of graces, as it is written in the wedding ceremony. The

Lord Jesus said I am not coming to destroy and put the Law aside. No, I come to elevate the person and elevate the Law to the statute of perfection.

Christ gives us many practical examples and He will give six reciprocal points between the Law and Jesus which we will talk about later in this series; "you have heard but I say to you".

What does God want to tell us here? He says, I will elevate the person from the level of an "eye for an eye" to the level of "love your enemy", I will elevate the person from the external appearances to the internal appearances. The commandments are very holy, but were difficult for a person to implement during the time of the Law, because God cannot ask from us, His children, the life of perfection unless it is during the era of grace, reconciliation, salvation and renewal. Before God asks me to love my enemy, bless those who curse you, do good to those who hate you, and pray for those who spitefully use and persecute you, He has to first equip us with a new, clean heart, supported by the Holy Spirit which dwells in us. Then, the Holy Spirit brings its fruits, which is love. Then I can say to my enemy "my beloved" and I can stand and pray for a person who insults me.

St. Paul understood perfectly the commandments and the thinking of Christ when He said, "But we have the mind of Christ" (1 Corinthians 2:16). St. Paul also said, "But when the kindness and the love of God our Saviour toward man appeared, not by works of righteousness which we have done, but according to His mercy He saved us, through the washing of regeneration and renewing of the Holy Spirit", not only that, but, "whom He poured out on us abundantly through Jesus Christ our Saviour" (Titus 3:4-7).

Jesus concludes this paragraph saying, as the key point, "Unless your righteousness exceeds the righteousness of the scribes and Pharisees, you will by no means enter the kingdom of heaven". Consider what Jesus wants to tell us here. He tells us that what's important is not the formalities, like the scribes and Pharisees considered important, thinking they were righteous (external appearances). Christ does not want false righteousness and boasting. We won't talk here about the woes which the Lord mentioned regarding the scribes and Pharisees, He really hammered them.

Our worship is not an external one of formalities, offering of sacrifices, self-righteousness, ticking the box or standing as a deacon on Sundays. It is not that. Jesus said, "My Son give Me your heart" (Proverbs 23:26). I need to show mercy not sacrifice, I need God's righteousness, I need grace to cover me and the Holy Spirit to renew my nature and then I can reach the heights of the Commandments and I will be elevated above the righteousness of the scribes and Pharisees.

Our Lord Jesus wants love, hearts full of love, "Now the purpose of the commandment is love from a pure heart, from a good conscience, and from sincere faith, from which some, having strayed, have turned aside to idle talk, desiring to be teachers of the law, understanding neither what they say nor the things which they affirm" (1 Timothy 1:5-7).

Jesus wants love from a pure heart, from within. He wants us to be a temple of the Holy Spirit, to dwell in us, to work in us, to be fruitful. The Spirit will work, we are not made perfect by the Law. The Lord said, "Are you so foolish? Having begun in the Spirit, are you now being made perfect by the flesh?" (Galatians 3:3). God wants to tell us today, "Care for your heart, purify your heart and offer it to Me so I can dwell in it and fill it, to rest in it".

> JESUS WANTS LOVE FROM A PURE HEART, FROM WITHIN.

St. Makarios the Great said, "So the heart will be a castle for the Lord Jesus". Stop focusing on the external appearances. Don't be trapped by this like the scribes and Pharisees were. You will not enter the Kingdom of God if you do not exceed their righteousness. Offer your heart to God, make it the manger for the birth of the Lord. Offer to Him your hearts, your life, just as the hymn said, "Rejoice Lord, we offer our hearts, our life". This is what our Lord wants from us today in these simple words.

My dear beloved, let us flee from external appearances. At times we want to show others and God how good we are? Don't be like the scribes and Pharisees, remember the "woe to you". Work on the internal, inside your heart. Nowadays, there are plenty showing external appearances, from inside and outside the church. God wants His righteousness to cover us.

Our Good Lord, our Holy Lord, we can't do this unless we come to You and offer our hearts to You. Grant us grace to offer our hearts and You cover us with Your grace and fill us with Your Spirit. To You is the glory and honour forever and ever. Amen.

The Prison of Unforgiveness

"First be reconciled to your brother, and then come and offer your gift. (Matthew 5:24)

In the previous sermon, we agreed that Jesus, after introducing us to the perfection of the commandment, elevates us to a new person, with a new heart and the regeneration of the Holy Spirit. Now, Jesus gives us six practical works.

The first is, "If you remember that your brother has something against you, leave your gift there before the altar, and go first to reconcile with your brother". A self-inflicted imprisonment is where the person enters with their own hands, closes the door on themselves and throws the key into the ocean; the prison of unforgiveness. This prison is full of people. It is very alarming that the person enters themselves, with their own will and closes the door on themselves and says, "I will not forgive", and the door will be shut. The key for that prison is forgiveness, you will find the door opens immediately.

How many people have we seen living with unforgiveness until the very end of their life? How many people live without peace because of this lack of forgiveness? Christ makes it very clear, He says, if you are upset with someone, don't approach the church or the altar, leave your offering, and go to your brother. The only time the church tells us not to have Holy Communion is when we don't have forgiveness for others. Many people colour it, shape it, decorated it and say, "No, I don't have anything in my heart towards this person, I just want to stay away". Many of us fall into this pattern, but the commandment of God enlightens our eyes from afar off. The Bible clearly tells us there is either black or white, there is no grey. People make this grey colour, mixing things together and end up with a new concept of Christianity. Everyone has a different concept, everyone translates or understands it according to their own mind. This reading from Matthew 5:21-26, shows us clearly what lack of forgiveness is. Christ

THE KEY FOR THAT PRISON IS FORGIVENESS, YOU WILL FIND THE DOOR OPENS IMMEDIATELY.

also speaks of this in Matthew 18:21-34 with the Parable of the Unforgiving Servant.

The greatest obstacle for unforgiveness is the EGO; the ego of the person which puts us in the prison of unforgiveness. How? When our ego is inflated, we don't tolerate insults or even a word of guidance or even to guide others. When our ego is simple, it is of no importance to us; if you are told to go this way, you say ok, or that way, ok, we consider ourselves the least of all the others, as simple as dough, soft, lenient and easily moved. But when the ego is hard, the person is inflexible and is not moved.

The prison of unforgiveness is the worst of all prisons, which one enters with their own mind. This person is always an unhappy person, lacking peace. It is easy to say, "I forgive you my brother", but some would prefer to carry out an investigation, "Why did you say that, why did you do this or that?" You get the feeling that there are conditions for the forgiveness. In contrast, Jesus, in all His meetings with people, never asked any questions, rather He said, "Go, your sins are forgiven", or "Sin no more".

When we receive the absolution after confession, our confession father puts the cross on our head, taps our shoulder and says, "My beloved, may the grace of God support you", no conditions have been asked for.

Hence, why do we need to do this with others, why place conditions on our forgiveness? I believe there will be many, God forbid, whom the door of heaven will be closed on them, due to lack of forgiveness of others.

We are still living in the flesh and have the chance to review ourselves and reconcile with others, asking to start all over again, to open a new chapter together or at least to greet one another, to kiss each other with good and pure intention. Why do we insist on staying in the prison of unforgiveness? Christ said, "Lest your adversary deliver you to the judge, the judge hand you over to the officer, and you be thrown into prison. Assuredly, I say to you, you will by no means get out of there till you have paid the last penny" (Matthew 5:25-26).

Our Good Lord, our Kind Lord, how much Lord you pardoned of us? So much, every day, every second of our life and Lord, I don't pardon or overlook a penny of my brother or sister. On this blessed day, grant us the grace to forgive, grant us to be like You and to have Your thoughts and be like You and forgive. To You is the glory and honour forever and ever. Amen.

The Sin of Lust

"But I say to you that whoever looks at a woman to lust for her has already committed adultery with her in his heart. (Matthew 5:27)

We agreed that Jesus said, "That unless your righteousness exceeds the righteousness of the scribes and Pharisees, you will by no means enter the kingdom of heaven". What we have read in these verses is the Seventh Commandment, "You shall not commit adultery". However, here our Lord Jesus highlights a very important point, that of lust. Whoever looks at a woman; it is not just any look. The greatest war we face today is that of lust, and it is accessible in every place. What is the problem of this lust?

It abolished our first father Adam, this is the entrance to the sin of lust. Where lust dwells, Satan dwells. Lust gives permission for the devil to dwell within my heart. When the devil lives in my heart, it becomes an evil heart. As we mentioned earlier, there are two kinds of hearts; the righteous heart and the evil heart. As lust continues and with many falls, weakness occurs. And as weakness continues, truce with the devil takes place.

The will dissolves and the inner revolt against lust weakens, which is what extinguishes the flame and grieves the Holy Spirit from within. There is another danger; the way I view myself begins to diminish. My self-worth lessens, as Joshua said, "We were like grasshoppers in our own sight" (Numbers 13:33), and we develop low self-esteem. I feel I am of no value and I lose the sonship and begin to work against God's plan. This is the result of lust. But God's plan for me is that He raises me to holiness, as we mentioned previously, He raises me for the perfection of the Law.

Desire makes Satan have a right over me and he takes control over me saying, "You follow me and your will is under me and you will do what I tell you to do".

The second problem of lust is that, in the long run, we know that lust and evil continue to increase in the world. That is, evil of 20 years ago is different from 40 years, from now and in 20 or 30 years to come. Meaning that the level of evil that our children are fighting is greater than that which we fought against, with the grace of God. If I cannot deliver to my children a living experience of victory with our Lord, if I do not sincerely embrace living a sacred life, visible to them, it will be difficult for them to overcome. With what weapon do I give them to fight with? Each of us needs to experience victory with Christ. Like Jacob when he wrestled with God and God said to him today your name will be Israel because you fought with God and Christ supports him

But there are things that I need to do for Christ to give me the key. Christ says, "If your right eye causes you to sin, pluck it out and cast it from you... if your right hand causes you to sin, cut it off and cast it from you"; these things symbolise the will, enthusiasm and decision-making. Dear readers, repentance, love and success need a decision to be taken. Everything in the world needs a decision and I take it by the grace of God who supports me.

The first step in the process of victory is to say, "No. Enough". The decision you take should be strong. So, if you begin to read an inappropriate book, throw it away. Or a picture, destroy it. Or a relationship, end it. Take action, this is the first step. Then start to experience wrestling with God in prayer, in fasting, in prostrations, in crying, until you win and say to God "unless you bless me I will not leave you". This is the greatest experience you can have in life and you will be crowned with victory and with the grace of God.

THE FIRST STEP IN THE PROCESS OF VICTORY IS TO SAY, "NO. ENOUGH". THE DECISION YOU TAKE SHOULD BE STRONG.

And this is the second experience of Christ in which He told us, "Unless your righteousness exceeds the righteousness of the scribes and Pharisees".

Our Good Lord, Holy, pure and all-Holy God, Lord, whose will and desire for us is to be saints just as You are Holy, give us Lord that we want repentance in our life. Give us a grace to make a decision to say NO, and be strong by not returning to lust and sin. For You is the glory and the honour forever and ever. Amen.

The Sin of Sexual Immorality

"But I say to you that whoever divorces his wife for any reason except sexual immorality causes her to commit adultery; and whoever marries a woman who is divorced commits adultery"
(Matthew 5:32)

This is a very sensitive commandment which I am not qualified to talk about. It is a topic which the Church and the great fathers can speak about. In this series, we are trying to draw closer to the mind of Christ, and we all agree that He elevates us from the level of the Law in the Old Testament to the level of grace in the New Testament.

In the Old Testament, enmity between humans and each other caused them to fall into sin. The human nature became corrupted between Adam and Eve. In Genesis, God looked for Adam and Eve but they fled from Him, they hid and tried to cover their nakedness and the Lord asked them, "Where are you?" At that instance, enmity started between mankind, who fell, and the Holy God who created them in His image and His likeness.

It is written, "And they heard the sound of the Lord God walking in the garden in the cool of the day, and Adam and his wife hid themselves from the presence of the Lord God among the trees of the garden. Then the Lord God called to Adam and said to him, "Where are you?" So, he said, "I heard Your voice in the garden, and I was afraid because I was naked; and I hid myself." And He said, "Who told you that you were naked? Have you eaten from the tree of which I commanded you that you should not eat?" (Genesis 3:8-11). This same voice always calls us, asking us, "where are you?"

Now begins the first conversation between Adam and Eve, "Then the man said, 'The woman whom You gave to be with me, she gave me of the tree, and I ate'. And the Lord God said to the woman, 'What is this you have done?' The woman said, 'The serpent deceived me, and I ate'". (Genesis 3:12-13).

This scene shows a fracture between the man and his wife. He put the blame on her and escaped his responsibility as a husband and a leader of the family. Where is the marital love? Gone, disappeared. Where is the picture of Jesus? Where is the new Adam? All gone. This is not the picture of Jesus.

Enmity between humans began to increase. Cain murdered his brother Abel; evil was at work and peace was lost between people. Our Lord had to come up with a new Law, a new covenant was introduced in the New Testament which was pivotal. The New Testament was built on this pivotal change, Salvation and the Kingdom of God. Everything is centred on Salvation and the Lord's plan to rescue mankind and to open the Kingdom to the whole of humanity, including the Sacrament of Marriage.

When the Pharisees asked the Lord Jesus, testing Him, "Is it lawful for a man to divorce his wife?". He answered with a question, "What did Moses command you?" They replied, "Moses permitted a man to write a certificate of divorce and to dismiss her". Jesus answered and said, "Because of the hardness of your hearts he wrote you this precept. But from the beginning of creation, God 'made them male and female'. 'For this reason, a man shall leave his father and mother and be joined to his wife, and the two shall become one flesh'; so, then they are no longer two, but one flesh. Therefore, what God has joined together, let not man separate." (Mark 10).

What is the significance of this? When the Kingdom opened, the Church began to practise the Sacrament of Marriage between a man and a woman for the Kingdom, so both of them and their children can enter the Kingdom of God.

So, unlike in the Old Testament, the marriage law is for enjoyment but also for the inheritance of the Kingdom and eternal life. Hence, in the Sacrament of Marriage, the young couple, in fact most of us, do not understand the sacred bond between the man and the woman, in accordance with being bound with the body of Christ; a mystery of the Holy Spirit working in the Church between the man and the woman to form a new entity.

In the prayer in the Sacrament of Marriage, the priest says, "The Father, the Son and the Holy Spirit, sanctify both of them". The Holy Spirit then dwells in the them and blesses them and forms a new entity, a new church which is formed between the man and the woman and their offspring for the Kingdom of God.

The man and the woman no longer have their own entity, but each one together makes a new entity, the entity of marriage, the holy one before God, for the Kingdom, through being bound with the body of Christ, by the power, blessing and work of the Holy Spirit, the possessor of this sacrament. Hence, at this point, the church honours the husband and the wife and tells them, "honour this sacrament and sanctify it for the Kingdom". It is for this reason our Lord Jesus Christ raised this sacrament and this commandment.

The old enmity between the man and the woman fell and the gap between God and us dissolved. We are no longer slaves with their master, but children with their father. With the enmity gone, we can say, "Our Father who are in heaven", a new small church is built.

Since the Church is subject to Christ and, after the Sacrament of Marriage, a new little church has been formed, we direct the woman, oh beloved daughter, submit to your husband as the Lord, for the husband is the head of the wife as Christ is head of the Church. Submission is not a form of humiliation, but just as the Church submits to Christ so the wife submits to her husband. Then the Church tells the husband, oh beloved son, Christ loves the Church and died for her, hence, from today onwards, you must love your wife as Christ loved the Church and died for her. This is the level asked for of the husband and wife. With this sacrament a new entity has been created and the Holy Spirit gathers the husband and the wife and enables them to fulfil the commandments and sacrifice, as Christ sacrificed Himself for the sake of our salvation.

> WE ARE NO LONGER SLAVES WITH THEIR MASTER, BUT CHILDREN WITH THEIR FATHER. WITH THE ENMITY GONE, WE CAN SAY, "OUR FATHER WHO ARE IN HEAVEN", A NEW SMALL CHURCH IS BUILT.

This is the rationale behind this sacrament and the thinking of our Lord Jesus Christ. Christ transformed the image of marriage in the New Testament, which was damaged by Adam and Eve.

Our Good Lord and our Holy Lord who sanctified and blessed everything. Bless our family, our children, our marriage. Bless Lord and sanctify this great sacrament in our life so we can be sanctified in You. To You be the glory and the honour, forever and ever. Amen.

You Shall Not Swear Falsely

"Again, you have heard that it was said to those of old, 'You shall not swear falsely, but shall perform your oaths to the Lord.'
(Matthew 5:33)

In the old days a person's word was their word, as the saying goes "a person is only as good as their word". In the early days of Christianity, a Christian was easily distinguished from others by their word, they do not go back on their word, it is like a contract. A Christian was known by the statement "believe me", their word was final and true. Christians were given the title ‘honest’. I think that word ‘integrity’ is the right word for this title. Integrity is like a golden coin, meaning that the person has the highest standards, unmatched by anyone. The true Christian lives by the standards of the Bible, one behaviour, one intention. There is no need to swear because every word that proceeds from their mouth is balanced on a fine scale. This was the early Christian person.

Is this the same image of a Christian in 2020? I think you may agree with me that this picture has changed and possibly, completely different. Nowadays, it is difficult to differentiate a Christian from everybody else, they are very similar, whether inside or outside the Church. The manner of speech, the use of bad language, insults, changing their word, playing with words and twisting them, being malicious. This is how to quench the Spirit. And unfortunately, our young children see all this before their very eyes from their parents. They have very sensitive cameras with enlarged zoom lenses. There is no more integrity. This is not the level that Christ came to elevate us to, “let your conduct be worthy of the Gospel of Christ” (Philippians 1:27), this is not the commandment; these are not the children of God.

Our message today is, let us consider our words, take care of every word we say, “But I say to you that for every idle word men may speak, they will give account of it in the day of judgment. For by your words you will be justified, and by your words you will be condemned.” (Matthew 12:36-37).

Let us reflect on why we have reached this level. We now have the wisdom of mankind, sensual, demonic, which are the things which now dominate the whole world. But the Lord said, "You are not of the world, if you are from the world, the world will know you, but we are his own, and am known by My own. My sheep hear My voice, and I know them, and they follow Me".

You are the salt, you are the light, you are different, yes, you and I, we are different. The Christian person must have a high level of integrity, their words must be honest and not changing, not coloured differently or shaped differently. We don't think "the goal justifies the means". This is not our way, but instead, the way of the world, the politician, the financial institution. But for us, we have the mind of Christ. We worship a living God who chooses us to be His own. Let us return to the right picture of what a Christian should be, starting with our own words, considering each word before we utter it. Start to refuse that thought and return back and say I am the image of God.

For nothing is secret that will not be revealed. We see people laugh. Many years ago, my father told me you can laugh at some people sometimes, you can laugh at all people sometimes but you cannot laugh at all people all the time. We see people plan tricks and are then are exposed.

> THE TRUE CHRISTIAN LIVES BY THE STANDARDS OF THE BIBLE, ONE BEHAVIOUR, ONE INTENTION.

The Christian is not like that, they are a salt and a light and they enlighten others. Search in your own world, start first in your own home, in your family. Change your world and make it different. Be honest in the little, don't swear at home, don't create false stories, and when God sees you honest and faithful in the little, He will make you faithful also in the big things. Purify your words, think before you speak, if you don't know something, say clearly, I don't know, if you don't know, don't talk, silence is great and powerful. Don't tell bad jokes or use bad words, don't criticise others so that you may reach this level of integrity.

Our Good Lord, Jesus Christ, who elevates us to the highest level of holiness and perfection, grant us a special salt and give us all salted words. To You is the glory and honour, forever and ever. Amen.

An Eye for an Eye and a Tooth for a Tooth

"..But I tell you not to resist an evil person. But whoever slaps you on your right cheek, turn the other to him also."
(Matthew 5:38)

Admittedly, this commandment is very hard. I pray that God grants us the grace to talk about this point. It is important to first accept it in our heart and to think seriously and let the Holy Spirit work in us.

Many people stand in front of this commandment, "Whoever slaps you on your right cheek, turn the other to him also". It is easy in theory but not in practice. We all agree that the Lord Jesus, to whom is the glory, never says theoretical words. All His words are spirit and life, "The words that I speak to you are spirit, and they are life" (John 6:63). So, you take it with the spirit and convert it to life. In life we see people live and they don't realise that they are alive. We see people live, but they don't know why they are living and we see people living and they know why they are living, it is not philosophy. Let me explain.

What makes people differ is the goal in their life. Life without a goal is meaningless. Once I know the goal of my existence on earth, everything becomes meaningful. Every action has a meaning.

On the surface it seems that these words of Christ are hard. He says difficult things which are above our capacity, "whoever slaps you on your right cheek, turn the other to him also. And whoever compels you to go one mile, go with him two, if any one wants to sue you and take away your tunic, let him have your cloak also". Hard. Lord, why are You asking these difficult things from us? Did You put us on this earth so that everyone can humiliate us? Is this the Christianity that You want us to live and abide by? But what is the message behind all these words?

What is the mind of Jesus in these series? Lord, what is Your thinking in us? God wants to tell us that you can't find meaning in life with your perspective of taking and enjoyment and pleasure. Once you see what the opposite of taking is, which is giving, life will have meaning. We would all agree that the times we gave more than we took, and the times we were selfless and not selfish, we discovered that we were very joyful and extremely happy.

St. Paul was transformed into a different person after he met our Lord Jesus Christ. He said, "But what things were gain to me, these I have counted loss for Christ. I press toward the goal for the prize of the upward call of God in Christ Jesus" (Philippians 3:7, 14); "And I will very gladly spend and be spent for your souls" (2 Corinthians 12:15); "We were well pleased to impart to you not only the gospel of God, but also our own lives" (Thessalonians 2:8); "For I could wish that I myself were accursed from Christ for my brethren" (Romans 9:3); "That you must support the weak. And remember the words of the Lord Jesus, that He said, 'It is more blessed to give than to receive'" (Acts 20:35).

Once one meets truly with the Lord, they begin to understand God clearly. This does not happen overnight. It is an immensely strong relationship between God and the individual who becomes enlightened by the grace of God and the work of the Holy Spirit, and starts to know the mind and the thinking of our Lord Jesus Christ.

Once I realise what the Lord needs me to do, I start to see that life is to give more than to take, more sacrifice, more love, more forgiveness and this will become your goal in life. It is just like a candle in the Church, it gives light all day long, it burns to give light, we forget it is there, but that doesn't matter because it lights and melts. Why are we fascinated by St. Abraam? Why do we love St. Bishoy so much, who sacrificed and carried the old monk on his shoulders? Why did the Lord Jesus bless the poor widow who put in two mites? All these examples have one thing in common, sacrifice. Our Lord said in the Gospel of St. John, "Unless a grain of wheat falls into the ground and dies, it remains alone; but if it dies, it produces much grain" (John 12:24).

> ONCE I REALISE WHAT THE LORD NEEDS ME TO DO, I START TO SEE THAT LIFE IS TO GIVE MORE THAN TO TAKE, MORE SACRIFICE, MORE LOVE, MORE FORGIVENESS AND THIS WILL BECOME YOUR GOAL IN LIFE.

Here, Christ wants to tell us, as long as the ego remains inside me and does not die, concentrating on the light of myself, my pleasures and my enjoyment in life, I will remain as a vase. But when the grain of wheat falls and dies, with the condition of accepting to die for the sake of Christ as Christ died for us, only then does it produce more grain.

How lucky is the person who sacrifices, how lucky is the person who knows their purpose in life, they will receive more blessings from God. Many of us search for enjoyment in life but are unable to find it until we reach God's plan and start living for the sacrifice of others, "Spend and be spent", the best words of St. Paul the Apostle.

Our Lord God and Saviour Jesus Christ, on this blessed day, give us the grain of wheat that falls and dies. Give us the grace so that we will be fruitful and have a goal in our life to light like the candle for all our surroundings. Give us to understand Your mind and Your thinking. To You is the glory and the honour, forever and ever. Amen.

You Shall Love Your Neighbour

"But I say to you, love your enemies, bless those who curse you, do good to those who hate you, and pray for those who spitefully use you and persecute you, that you may be sons of your Father in heaven"
(Matthew 5:43-48)

I pray to God that these words touch my heart first. I know that many of us will hear these words and say, "These words definitely do not apply to me". Let us agree on some principles regarding our spiritual life. There is a difference between the teachings of our Lord Jesus Christ and what He asks of me and the level that I reach. But this is the level that our Lord Jesus wants from us in the New Testament. If I can't reach this level it means my spiritual life is weak and we will discuss this now.

Consider the following example: An exam paper for a particular subject has a particular question. If I am unable to answer the question then it is I who did not study and therefore could not answer the question. It is then my fault and my problem. I think now it may be a little clearer. It is not an option to not answer the question, because, if I don't answer it, it will make the difference in heaven. Ask God to open our hearts and grant us a special grace to understand what is required of us. Our aim is to understand the mind of Christ, by knowing His mind we will know what is required of us in the commandment. It seems that this commandment is hard but God's commandments are not hard.

The Lord Himself showed love towards His enemies on the Cross. We have His example to live by. Likewise, St. Stephen was filled with the Holy Spirit. So, the Lord's commandments are for those who are filled with the Holy Spirit. This is the first important point; that God's commandments are simple and easy if we are filled with the Holy Spirit and believe in His work.

THE LORD HIMSELF SHOWED LOVE TOWARDS HIS ENEMIES ON THE CROSS. WE HAVE HIS EXAMPLE TO LIVE BY.

The teachings of the Early Church Fathers tell us that there is a way to life and a way to death. There is a huge difference between the two ways, for life is to love God, who created you to love your neighbour as yourself and everything and whatever you want done to you, do to others.

The Christian will make a difference when they bless those who insult them, pray for their enemies and fast for those who persecute them; not so that God takes revenge on them but for God to gain them to His own.

The Great St. Ignatius of Antioch, who was martyred at the beginning of the 2nd Century, wrote in his Epistle to the Ephesians, "Your faith is what lifts you up, but love is the way you ascend to God".

So, you and I, with the drop of love that we offer and collect in our lamps with the wise virgins, is the way that leads us to God. If we think there is another way to God other than to love Him and to love all people, then we will never reach heaven, we will be going the wrong way.

Christ said pray without ceasing for all those who insult you, annoy you, humiliate you, disapprove of you. He said it is like a race, the best are those who carry the injustice and humiliation. So, what is required of us? St. Ignatius also said that what distinguishes a Christian from others is their conduct, their language, their habits and a way of living which deserves admiration and acknowledgement. As citizens, they participate in everything but they are strangers. They bear all things, they are present in flesh but they are not living for the flesh. They spend their days on earth, but they are linked to the heavenly homeland. They love all people but are persecuted by them. They are slandered by people but they excuse these people. They are sworn at but they bless those who swear at them. They are insulted but they give honour to others. They do good but are rewarded by evil. When they are punished by death, they rejoice as if they are resurrected for life. The Jews fought them as if they were foreigners and the Greeks oppressed them. Nevertheless, those who hate them are unable to express the reason for their hatred.

This is the Christian whom the Lord described and thought about in His words and teachings. This is the Christian whom the Lord gave the ability to live as salt and light. This is God's plan for you and for me.

The question now is, do you want to live according to God's plan or do you want to have your own plan, according to your own mind, with your own teachings and your own thoughts. Do you want to be like Christ, who carried His cross and follow Him, whose name is calming to you, and you enjoy His power and His blessings and gifts? Or do you want to live a worldly, materialistic life? This life would lead to a different end. One way leads to life and the other does not.

The question which God gives us today is what do you want? Do you want to live according to God's plan or according to your own will? We will continue....

You Shall Love Your Enemies

In the previous sermon we ended with a question, "do we need to live according to God's plan or according to our own mind?"

This question is very important and we need to ask it several times a day. If I want to live according to God's plan, I need to love my enemies and bless them, in order to be the child of my Father who is in Heaven. God enables us to surpass human ability and love our enemy and bless those who curse us and pray for those who offend us. Here comes the shortage of loving others, as we are only able to love those around us and sometimes we are not even able to love them, our neighbour or those who are in the church, we find many excuses.

Remember my friend that the essence of Christianity is that our Lord came to change many things in our mind, in our personality, our self, our teaching and our practice.

In the days before Christ, people only loved those around them, that is why the lawyer asked Jesus, "Who is my neighbour?". Our Lord gave an excellent example of the Good Samaritan. In this parable, Christ changed, extended and expanded love for others regardless of colour, religion or belief. He said, help anyone, feed and care for anyone. He opened a huge gate of love and service. We ask, "Why are we not extending this love to others?"

Here are some answers:

The weakness of the Spirit in us. We do not take advantage of the existing capabilities.

We do not ask for it. We accept defeat; hence we do not benefit.

The ego is the obstacle that prevents our spiritual growth. When we neglect the ego, it will be easy to extend love to others or at least have the feeling of reconciliation.

When we talk about the love of enemy, let us differentiate between the emotional love and loving will. Emotional love is the love a husband has for his wife and a wife has for her husband or a mother has for her children. The loving will is what the Lord asks from us, "You shall love the Lord your God with all your heart, with all your soul, and with all your mind" (Deuteronomy 6:5). When we reach this point, then we will be able to love our enemies because the love will flow from a heart filled with God.

Likewise, "Bless he who curses you"; in order to accept this, we must be part of Christ who accepted the curse on the Cross. This means I must be a strong partner, immersed in Christ, filled with Him and resemble Him. When I consider this commandment with my own efforts in mind, or my own might or power, I will never reach it. It is not through human efforts that I attain this but, on the contrary, if I am filled with the Lord Jesus and with His Spirit, the unlimited in capacity, then the Lord will grant me love for my enemies and the ability to bless them.

Here are some practices on how to love your enemy:

St. John Chrysostom tells us to start with something very small until the Lord grants you the most.

If someone offends you, don't offend them back and don't think of taking revenge on them, "'Vengeance is Mine, I will repay,' says the Lord". (Romans 12:19).

Pray for those who offend you. Prayer solves many things. Ask the Lord to guide you and those who offend you and to reduce your anger. Hence, prayer benefits you and your offender.

Forgive those who offend you and leave the whole matter before God. Be alert to the ways of the devil, who always magnifies the problem. Say to yourself and the offender, "I forgive you", because in the Lord's Prayer, He asks us to forgive.

Completely forget and, if the devil reminds you or aggravates you, say, "The Lord rebuke you!", just as Archangel Michael said to the devil.

Try to find excuses for those who offend you just as the Lord said, "Father, forgive them, for they do not know what they do."

Try to offer help or service to those who offend you so that their understanding towards you is altered and so that they feel loved and not hated, just as the Lord said, "Do good to those who hate you". By asking after them, these simple words or this kind act may melt the ice between you and them.

Don't wait for others to apologise, but start first by going to them and opening your heart to them, just as the father did for the prodigal son. The Lord Jesus goes to the sinner and knocks on their door. So, you will resemble the Lord who always seeks us out.

Try to reach the level where your heart is filled with love for everyone. Don't differentiate, love all and remember the words of our Lord, "This is My commandment, that you love one another as I have loved you. Greater love has no one than this, than to lay down one's life for his friends". (John 15:12-13).

TRY TO FIND EXCUSES FOR THOSE WHO OFFEND YOU JUST AS THE LORD SAID, "FATHER, FORGIVE THEM, FOR THEY DO NOT KNOW WHAT THEY DO."

In summary, although it is a difficult commandment and quite a high level to reach, we are obliged to be perfect. How long will we stay as we are without changing, putting this commandment aside like a difficult exam which we don't want to touch or try to avoid?

This is the aim of this series; to get our minds thinking of our direction, our life, our way. Everyone wants to stay in their own way but I hope these simple words can affect us all and create enough zeal in us to change.

Our Good Lord, our Holy Lord, on this blessed day, we confess to You our weakness before this commandment of 'love', almost paralysed in it. We don't have energy, or power, or desire, but You Lord came to change everything and to dissolve all the gaps and to teach us to have the true love like the Good Samaritan. Give us grace to love, sacrifice and spend and be spent as You did. To you is the glory and the honour, forever and ever. Amen.

Faith, Hope, Love

Before we continue with our contemplations, allow me to make further comments on the previous two commandments of "love your enemies, bless those who curse you". I would like to begin with a true story:

In the year 2002 in the USA, there was a man by the name of Ridgway, who was a serial killer and was convicted of murdering 48 women. The court announced a closure which would gather the parents of all the victims to confront the killer before sentencing him to death. As each family member appeared before the guilty man, the judge asked "are you guilty of this crime" and in each case his reply was, "I am guilty". His face remained expressionless. The parents of each victim cried, insulted him, expressed hate for him, swore at him, wished him hell and to suffer like they are suffering for the loss of their loved ones. He heard all these words with no reply until the final victim's family member, stood before him. He was an elderly man and he stood before the killer and said the following words, "Mr. Ridgway, the whole room is filled with people who hate you, insulted you, even cursed you, but my Christ teaches me differently. He teaches me to love my enemy and to forgive those who wrong me and, because of my Christ, I forgive you". Once the killer heard these words, he broke down and cried and spoke emotional words due to this act of forgiveness.

Whilst this is an extreme example, I ask the question, "what are our assets?" Money? No. Our property? No. What then? The Lord tells us there are three things in the Bible: Faith, Hope, Love. St. Paul says, "But the greatest of these is Love". Love is our asset in this world. Do you want to know if you are rich or poor? Then check how much love you have in your heart. The rich person has a heart full of love. If your heart is empty of love then, unfortunately, you are a wicked person in this world.

Love is our asset in this world. Do you want to know if you are rich or poor? Then check how much love you have in your heart.

In the Book of Revelation, the angel said, "I have this against you that you have left..." What is it? Your money, your assets? No. He said, "You have left your first love". (Revelation 2:4). God cannot build on you if you don't have love. You must repent first, "Remember therefore from where you have fallen, repent and do the first works". (Revelation 2:5).

Love is not an easy commandment but this is what our Christianity is all about. If we have no love in our life then we have not understood anything at all. It is like a student who studied for an exam but was given a different question to what they studied and they received zero.

What is the most famous verse in the whole world? 3:16. We can say this without even saying the book it is in, "For God so loved the world that He gave His only begotten Son, that whoever believes in Him should not perish but have everlasting life" (John 3:16). The pivotal word in this verse is LOVE.

Christ asks of us, at all times, to love. He spoke His great commandment, "The first of all the commandments is: 'Hear, O Israel, the Lord our God, the Lord is one. And you shall love the Lord your God with all your heart, with all your soul, with all your mind, and with all your strength.' This is the first commandment. And the second, like it, is this: 'You shall love your neighbour as yourself.' There is no other commandment greater than these." (Mark 12:29-31). For the whole world to smell My aroma, you must love one another, "By this all will know that you are My disciples, if you have love for one another." (John 13:35).

In St. Paul's famous chapter on love, 1 Corinthians 13, he mentions 14 points on what love is. The great, wide and easy gate to enter heaven is love, while the very narrow gate to enter heaven is lack of love and forgiveness. St. Paul tells us that if I have not love I am nothing, "Though I speak with the tongues of men and of angels, but have not love, I have become sounding brass or a clanging cymbal. And though I have the gift of prophecy, and understand all mysteries and all knowledge, and though I have all faith, so that I could remove mountains, but have not love, I am nothing. And though I bestow all my goods to feed the poor, and though I give my body to be burned, but have not love, it profits me nothing." (1 Corinthians 13:1-3). This is the great commandment, the king of laws, the key to heaven. If you have love, then you get the key to heaven and happiness. The Bible tells us without love we are blind.

How can I attain this love? Each time you try with your own efforts you will not succeed. You will not know the means, you will be wasting your time and will eventually be discouraged. You may have already experienced being rejected by someone, or tried to reconcile with someone, or attempted to give love and it did not succeed. It can be very hurtful. How, therefore, can we get this love? Consider the beautiful words in Isaiah 55:1, "Everyone who thirsts, come to the waters; and you who have no money, come, buy and eat. Yes, come, buy wine and milk without money and without price." Free. God said, come and I will fill you who are thirsty for the Holy Spirit. I want to give you what your heart desires. He is searching for vessels to fill.

So, what do I need to do?

Ask in prayer: "God fill me, I am thirsty, fill me with your Holy Spirit and fill me till I overflow".

God never fills and overflows on a corrupted land, unclean, impure. That is why He said, "Remember therefore from where you have fallen; repent and do the first works". (Revelation 2:5). There is no other way than repentance. Do not go around the door of repentance as the Israelites did, staying in the wilderness for 40 years.

Offer a true repentance from the heart, with remorse and tears. Be humble in your actions, don't have pride when dealing with others. What are you proud of? Why do you focus on yourself? The Holy Spirit dwells in a meek person, therefore, be humble and be a disciple of an experienced person and when your spirituality is low, say so, don't be embarrassed. In the real world, if you were bankrupt, you would not be embarrassed to say so. Don't show off and be a hypocrite. Stand before God. Pray and ask Him, "Lord, my spirituality is low, fill me with the fruit of love, from Your Spirit so that I can be filled and give me grace to forgive from the depth of my heart and grant me grace in the eyes of others to accept me.

What happens if I do all this but people still don't accept me? Ask again and continue trying, all these trials are not overlooked by God. You will find God lifting you up high. The person who tries and has been rejected has a high rank in God's eyes.

What happens if you are the person who has rejected that love which was extended by someone else and your heart is hardened and you still don't want to give them a chance? We tell you to check yourself, you are in great danger and you will lose everything that you do without love and without forgiveness.

Heaven is great and deserves all your efforts to gain it. Always keep your eyes on it, don't waste it on idle things.

On this blessed day, we lift up our hearts and say, Our Lord of love, who commanded us to love, who loved us till the end, till death, fill us with Your Spirit, give us to love and to not give up, help us to follow the way of love that you walk through, help us to love and to love till our last breath. To You is the glory and the honour, forever and ever. Amen.

Complete your Charitable Deeds in Secret

"Take heed that you do not do your charitable deeds before men, to be seen by them. Otherwise you have no reward from your Father in heaven.
(Matthew 6:1)

After establishing His new teachings in Chapter 5 and laying down the basic principles for us, Christ continues in

Chapter 6 to explain the true, genuine worship, that comes from the heart, the undivided worship which has the goal of establishing a very real, personal and strong relationship with our Heavenly Father. Christ divides worship into two types of acts: the first, in which there is a service such as preaching or evangelism, which are considered beacons of the Church, and are visible to all and cannot be hidden because they contain the glory of our Lord. And the second act, is private worship such as fasting, vigilance, prayer and prostrations. This pure, heartfelt worship does not benefit from being openly displayed and not seen before any human being. Christ says, "But you, when you pray, go into your room, and when you have shut your door, pray to your Father who is in the secret place; and your Father who sees in secret will reward you openly" (Matthew 6:6).

Worship with God is the basis and the centre of the sacred life of communion between us and our Heavenly Father. Everything we offer in it are sacrifices of love in which we express our love for Him, our submission, our fear of Him and our obedience to Him, in order to form a relationship and fellowship through the Holy Spirit with our Heavenly Father. Every time we enter and talk we enter and talk to the Lord, we pour ourselves into prayer, prostrations and thus, the soul will be fulfilled. Our soul becomes fruitful and satisfied, not needing anything from anyone. However, at times, a deviation occurs, and the purpose is deviated, so the goal also deviates. This comes from poverty within the soul, and drought occurs and does not take comfort in God and then the individual begins to beg. They begin to take comfort from others and enters into hypocrisy. Christ warns us about this. What is hypocrisy? We all, without exception, have a part of hypocrisy and we all master it; however, it varies from person to person.

The origin of the word hypocrisy is 'acting out' or 'playing out'. It comes from the theatre, like acting, meaning one pretends to be a different shape or form from what they really are. Internal, heartfelt worship is not like external worship, that is, it does not have two sides. As we have already said, it begins as deviation or perversion and the more serious problem of ambivalence and is difficult to repent from and return to God. This sort of person is condemned by Christ and we all know the woes that the Lord Jesus said about the scribes and Pharisees. And He said to the disciples, "Take heed and beware of the leaven of the Pharisees and the Sadducees" (Matthew 16:6). The leaven represents hypocrisy and there is nothing concealed that must be revealed. This disease may afflict any person, as St. Peter was afflicted with it as was St. Barnabas which you can read about in Galatians Chapter 2.

What are the causes of hypocrisy? Is it the feeling of inferiority? Do you want to appear like others? Do you want to reach a certain goal quickly without too much effort? Are you more concerned with outward appearances rather than looking after the inside?

And He said to them, "Woe to you, scribes and Pharisees, hypocrites! For you are like whitewashed tombs which indeed appear beautiful outwardly, but inside are full of dead men's bones and all uncleanness" (Matthew 23:27). I criticize others although I also do wrong. I see something that I want to fix in others but it is in me too. So, this is hypocrisy. I do much more worship when I am seen by people than when people do not see me. I attend church for long periods of time but when I am at home I do not pray or read my Bible, my room becomes cold from lack of prayers. I appear to be spiritually greater than I really am in order to ascend to great heights and receive glory and honour from people.

There is another kind of hypocrisy where one speaks a lot of spiritual matters but their heart is lukewarm or even cold and their heart is far from God, “These people draw near to Me with their mouth, and honour Me with their lips, but their heart is far from Me” (Matthew 15:8).

It is a yeast that enters inside the heart without knowing it, like a virus that enters the heart without your knowledge. St. Paul said, “Let love be without hypocrisy” (Romans 12:9), because there is such a thing as love in hypocrisy. How? These are many, like when we accept a kiss or say you are welcome, or you are worthy my beloved and all sorts of good things between one another but on the inside, they cannot stand each other and tell many stories about each other.

In today’s message, Christ warned of hypocrisy because it corrupts all spiritual life. How then do I resist hypocrisy? The first thing is to uncover it before our Lord, repent of it, and reveal it to your confession father. There are many sins which we confess and don’t say in detail but this one you must, so as to expose yourself.

The life of faith is our belief in our Lord, His love and mercy, with His knowledge, confident that He will surely hold my hand, step by step. There is no need to pretend a life of righteousness and piety when you do not have them. You can reach the depth, love and sacrifice of a spiritual life without hypocrisy.

Ask and pray to the Lord to remove this hypocrisy. Give us your wisdom Lord, give us Your Spirit Lord to keep us away from hypocrisy. In your prayers, always ask the Holy Spirit. Take the lives, deeds, faith and sayings of the saints and follow their example, because this is the way to holiness and perfection, to which God calls us. And we pray that God removes from us this hypocrisy which spoils our spiritual life.

> CHRIST WARNED OF HYPOCRISY BECAUSE IT CORRUPTS ALL SPIRITUAL LIFE.

Our Good Lord, our Kind Lord, you know how weak we are. You are the creator and sometimes we fall into hypocrisy. Give us grace to have love without hypocrisy and to aim, in prayer, to reach You, to have a holy, secret bond in our room and in our heart with You and in You. To You is the glory and the honour, forever and ever. Amen.

Pray in Secret

"But you, when you pray, go into your room, and when you have shut your door, pray to your Father who is in the secret place;" (Matthew 6:6)

I will start with a story: A Russian farmer, who worked hard and was very active, would come home from work to find his wife waiting for him, with a meal prepared. He would eat the meal and go to bed early because he had to wake up early the next morning to go to the fields and start work again. One day he was told to go home quickly because his wife was very sick. He rushed home and found her with a high fever. He put her in the carriage and rushed her to the nearest hospital in the village. Whilst they were in the carriage he kept saying I am sorry, I worked too much and did not spend time with you or communicate much with you, but from now on our life will be different. However, unfortunately, as he reached the hospital he discovered that his wife had passed away.

I am telling you this sad story to show that sometimes, while we live our lives, we do not communicate our feelings and emotions with God, nor do we reciprocate our love to Him. Our lives may end without really talking to or knowing God, just like this farmer who did not get to know his wife.

Today's message is about prayer, as we say, prayer destroys mountains. What is prayer? Prayer is something which is embedded in our nature. It is a call from God to be in His presence at all times. Prayer is *the* connection between God and us. So, whenever we pray we are really responding to His call. The most important point is for our soul to stand in the presence of its Creator. It is amazing that God descends to us, to listen and to answer our prayers. God wants us to talk to Him. He yearns for our communication. So, we are always invited by God to pray. Prayer is an act and it is complicated, as we shall see later. Hosea also said it is to please the human soul.

> PRAYER IS THE CONNECTION BETWEEN GOD AND US.

Prayer can be in a group, like when we pray the Liturgy at Church, it can be between two people praying together for someone in need, "For where two or three are gathered together in My name, I am there in the midst of them." (Matthew 18:20). And finally, the most important prayer is between you (alone) and God, in your room, where no one can see you or hear you, or feel you. This is where you expose your feelings, thoughts, sins, emotions, desires, dreams, disappointments and tears before God. Who of us is without hurt, sins, anxieties or has a sinful bondage of some kind? Who of us is not sad or feeling down or afraid of the future?

Consider the following example: Suppose you have many different coloured bobbins of thread which are all tangled up in a ball. Who is courageous enough to untangle this ball? Now, our lives, with all their problems and difficulties, are tangled together just as the ball of bobbins mentioned above. Only God, through prayer, can untangle this ball of different threads. These threads are our difficulties and life problems. The first thing that God gives us through prayer is PEACE. You feel that you have covered a long track in faith, you receive a great deal of comfort and the Holy Spirit fills you according to your needs. Sometimes the Spirit gives you joy and at other times, rebukes you for your sins. Another time gives you love and another time gives you condemnation. Prayer reduces conflict between people. So, the person that you have despised in the past, you now begin to like or you may even pray for.

In prayer we put all our troubles at the feet of our Lord Jesus. The successful prayer always leads to repentance and confession before God, without hypocrisy or shame and without being sugar coated. Perhaps in front of people we become ashamed of exposing our inner self but not in front of God. Every time we pray we grow our spiritual muscles in the same way we do our bodily muscles when we exercise. We need to wrestle with God to bless us. Through prayer our needs are satisfied, we stop begging for compassion, love or mercy from others. Thus, through prayer, all our needs are met and God saturates us. When you pray you will know the truth about yourself, and you know who you are and whom you stand in front of? And you discover your depth.

The Holy Spirit will fill you during prayer. Ask God to fill you. St Luke tells us, "How much more will your heavenly Father give the Holy Spirit to those who ask Him!" (Luke 11:13). Those who pray know what God's plan for them is, you will know your aim in life. Prayer will sanctify your heart from every sin, it gives you a good, heart of flesh and you will have a good relationship with God, so that when you meet Him you will be familiar with Him. See how much we lose when we neglect prayer. The most important thing in prayer is to have discipline; not saying I will pray when I feel like it.

The spiritual life is like being in the army; a soldier cannot exercise whenever he feels like it. He must have time for everything, for practice and exercise, otherwise, if he is attacked by the enemy, he will be defeated. The same goes for prayer, it is good to have someone to guide you such as your confession father and ask him to make a plan for you to learn how to pray. At the very least, you can pray in the morning and at night to meet with God.

God gave us many examples; He Himself prayed. He often retreated into the mountains and prayed. Before He chose the disciples, He prayed, or before He did anything. Before He went to the cross He prayed and said to us, "You always ought to pray and not lose heart" (Luke 18:1). Now

He wants us to pray so that there is a connection between Him and us. God does not need our prayers," You are not in need my servitude but it is I who needs Your Lordship". But prayer is a mutual sacrifice of love. He calls us by His love and we accept it with love.

Talking about prayer is endless. The fathers have mastered it. Our righteous and holy God, give us a heart that knows you like Peter and the strongest love of John's. Lord, give me a spiritual revolution that strengthens and raises me from weakness, heals me from a sick heart within me. I am the beggar, enrich me with your love so that I do not need to beg for love and compassion from others. Saturate me with Your love.

Make me like a dough in Your hands, to be a good bowl, full of love, forgiveness, honesty, and a contrite heart. Let my heart be according to Yours. Even when I stand before You I will not have empty hands, but I stand with a pure heart, full of love, repentance, kindness and bow to You with full reverence and submission. I am in Your hands O Lord, do what You want to do with me. To You is the glory and the honour, forever and ever. Amen.

Our Father Who Art in Heaven

After Christ told His disciples not to "use vain repetitions as the heathen do" (Matthew 6:7), *but rather, when you pray, say the Lord's Prayer.*

We say the Lord's Prayer often; in church, at home, on the road, or before a meal. This is good, but we often do not understand what we are saying and we repeat it. God, in this prayer, taught us how to talk to Him and how to enter into His presence. You will notice it has 7 requests:

The first half belongs to God and His glory, "Hallowed be Your name. Your Kingdom come. Your will be done". "Our Father who art in heaven", it describes a heart lifted towards heaven. This heaven can be your heart, that the Lord dwells in and it can be the heaven which the Lord dwells in. In both cases it is a state of raising the heart and preparing it to stand before God. It is a heart prayer; a profound prayer which carries all our needs.

The greatest thing that humanity, you and I, have gained is "Our Father". How great is the glory and the rich grace that we are able to say to the Creator to whom is the glory, "Our Father"? These words "Our Father" bring us into the presence of the Lord. He did not ask us to address Him as "Our Creator", "Our God", "Our Lord", but He gave us the words "Our Father".

If we were to meet any great person, we would have to go through their secretary first and make an appointment, but not our Lord. We call Him "Our Father", a relationship of a child and a true Father, although God has many qualities such as Judge and Creator. He said, when you pray, to call Him Father, the spirit of His children. He is my very own, personal, heavenly Father. How much honour, glory and treasure He has given us. God hears, attends and listens to every word we pray.

We are invited to a precious, holy event, to be in His presence and participate with all the heavenly celestial beings and the principalities who say, "Holy, Holy, Holy". They don't say "Our Father", but we, the wicked ones on this earth, full of corruption, the sinners, stand and raise our hands, making the sign of the cross and say, "Our

Father". What an honour is this Lord? What an enormous grace is this Lord?

I wish for us that we benefit today with one thought, teach us Lord how to talk to you as a child, give me a special grace on this blessed day, to live as your child and feel the sonship and to feel the affiliation to a great Father of all humanity, to You God, because often I do not understand this invitation, and I live like a slave outside the house and You asked me to be Your child to live inside the house.

The Pakistani lady, Balquis El Sheikh, converted to Christianity from Islam because of the words "Our Father". She wrote a book called, "I Dared To Call Him Father". This was the turning point in her journey to Christianity. It was the first time she saw God, whom she previously knew as the avenger and the feared one, as a Father, a beautiful, kind God. He is my Father, only mine, when I enter my room and call Him my Father. And this is why she became a Christian.

God calls us in many verses in the Bible. We say Our Father and He says My son, my son give Me your heart, My son keep My words, hear, my son, and be wise. In many verses God calls us to be His children, not a slave. And the beautiful verse, "No longer do I call you servants, for a servant does not know what his master is doing; but I have called you friends" (John 15:15). But sometimes we respond differently, like the verse in Isaiah, "For the Lord has spoken: 'I have nourished and brought up children, and they have rebelled against Me'" (Isaiah 1:2). Sometimes our reaction to our heavenly Father is not feeling His presence, so I leave the house and go to a far place like what the Prodigal son did. But my Father waits for me, looks everywhere, knocks on every door, knocks on my heart until I return, with regret, wounded, bruised. In spite of all this my Father is happy to see me and says to slaughter the fatted calf for me because, my son was dead and is alive again.

So please come now, I know these words will not last long, the human being forgets quickly. But nevertheless, I say, come, train yourself today, this week or this month, according to God's grace. When you pray and say "Our Father", stand for a while after saying these words, do not rush or run away quickly, but take your time. It is not homework but, "Delight yourself also in the Lord, and He shall give you the desires of your heart" (Psalm 37:4). Say "Our Father", then remain silent. Our Father wishes for such a thing, to enjoy standing in His presence saying "Our Father, My Father, My beloved".

When you pray these words, let them come from your heart, with an assurance, with confidence, knowing that you are a son or daughter, not a slave. You have a precious invitation. God lifts us higher and higher above all expectations and explanations. You are not a slave, you are My beloved son and My beloved daughter.

> WHEN YOU PRAY THESE WORDS, LET THEM COME FROM YOUR HEART, WITH AN ASSURANCE, WITH CONFIDENCE, KNOWING THAT YOU ARE A SON OR DAUGHTER, NOT A SLAVE.

My heavenly Father, I thank You. There are no words to express this gratitude when I stand before You and call You Father, my special, heavenly Father. I wish Lord to live on the level of sonship. I wish Lord to be inside the house not outside, not to live as a slave but as a child. Give us the grace to feel this sonship and the glory and the honour that You raised us up by Your incarnation. I thank You so much for this grace. Let me feel this beautiful taste and enjoy it in my mouth when I call You Father.

You are Our Father and the Father of all humanity and the Father of every person, from every race and every colour and every shape. This makes all humanity closer to us because each of us says, "Our Father". You are the Father of the orphan, the weak, the poor, the rich, of everyone. We thank You Lord. To You is the glory and the honour, forever and ever. Amen.

For where Your Treasure is, there Your Heart Will be Also

"Do not lay up for yourselves treasures on earth, where moth and rust destroy" (Matthew 6:19)

These words make us weary thinking about our treasure on earth and our treasure in heaven, but they are precious words which compel us to consider why Jesus spoke them. However, the question remains, why did He say them?

I will tell you a nice story which one of my beloved friends shared with me. He recalled that one day he was visiting someone at a hospital in Sydney. On his way, he passed by a homeless man. This man did not ask for anything, but my friend, feeling compassion for him, reached into his pocket and pulled out a coin and gave it to him. My friend added that he could not forget the smile on the face of this homeless man. They began to introduce each other and share each other's names. My friend continued on his way to finish his hospital visit. On his way back to his car he saw the homeless man on the other side of the road. With a loud voice the man called out to him by name and thanked him again. He was very happy. The value of the coin was not much but it made someone happy. This is the reason why Christ said, we should not have treasures on earth.

Is saving money considered wrong in Christianity? Absolutely not, but Christ always directs us to the correct path, which is to lay up our treasures in heaven not on earth.

However, accumulating money as a life's goal is unacceptable for the following reasons:

It indicates that the person who is doing this is worried or afraid for the future and considers their future will be secure by saving money, not by God's hand. Christ guarantees our lives on earth as well as our eternal life. He does not want us to depend on anything but God Himself.

If we are rich, it is possible that we become exposed to many lusts (body, eyes, pride); as the money increases so too does the desire to enjoy the materialistic things in life and one may begin to adore money,

> ❋
>
> Christ guarantees our lives on earth as well as our eternal life. He does not want us to depend on anything but God Himself.

neglecting one's spiritual life. Let us recall the Parable of the Rich Fool. This man said to himself, "I will do this: I will pull down my barns and build greater, and there I will store all my crops and my goods. And I will say to my soul, 'Soul, you have many goods laid up for many years; take your ease; eat, drink, and be merry'" (Luke 12:18-19). But God said to him, "Fool! This night your soul will be required of you; then whose will those things be which you have provided?" (Luke 12:20).

As one becomes richer, their dignity becomes higher in their own eyes as well as in the society. Observe how a rich man and a poor man is treated. The rich man is given honour, others bow down to them due to their money. The consequences; that person may lose Christ's goal for their life on earth and begin to think only of themselves and lose their feelings for others. How can they feel the poverty of others if they are rich? How can they understand that there are some people who do not have the essentials and necessities of life (food, clothes, medicine, a place to live, education and so on)? For sure they will not be able to relate to the sufferings of others. As a result, the rich person may become selfish or have no understanding of the pain of others. As their money increases their love of the world increases and begins to believe that their eternal life is on earth.

Earth is not our future. Christ said, "They are not of the world, just as I am not of the world" (John 17:16). This world will vanish, but our world is in heaven. One day I will leave this world whether I want to or not. Our destiny is heaven. We are strangers and are not of this world. As we say in the Divine Liturgy, "And we too, the foreigners in this world, preserve us in Your faith and grant us Your peace till the end".

Most importantly our Lord Jesus wants us to know that it is our poor brothers and sisters who give the blessings, not the rich who bless the poor. Yes, the rich take the blessings from the poor. He gives us the chance to take this blessing.

The following is a contemplation from one of the fathers regarding this point: We have a secret bank on earth which is called the bank of God's Kingdom. Each donation you give on earth (to the poor, sick, homeless and so on) is transferred to that bank, which accordingly is transferred to heaven in your eternal life, carrying the signature or the stamp of Jesus Christ.

Now we can more clearly understand what Jesus meant when He said, "Do not lay up for yourselves treasures on earth". Jesus concludes today's message with, "For where your treasure is, there your heart will be also".

Christ wants to put us before an exam and tries to see where we are, where our treasure is, where our hopes are, our thoughts, our hearts? Where is your heart concentrated on? Is it on earth or in heaven? Examine your heart and contemplate on how you deal with money. Is money the assurance of your life on earth? Does money protect you and your life? Do you feel safe in proportion to how much money you have? Or is Christ your goal? Christ does not want our treasure to be from the dust of the earth, but He wants our heart to be full of love, sympathy and mercy for our fellow human beings. The weak brothers and sisters. Who are my brothers and sisters? Everyone on earth. Look to the Good Samaritan and take him as an example to know who your neighbour is.

Our Good God, our Lord Jesus Christ, give us this day the grace to know that the money you gave us is to be used to help others in their needs. And that we should not think or calculate how much we spend on tithe or how much we donate, just donate generously. Lord, give us the blessing to discover the reality of our hearts, if it is from earth or hearts looking up towards the eternal life. To You is the glory and honour, forever and ever.

Amen.

The Lamp of the Body is the Eye

"The lamp of the body is the eye. If therefore your eye is good, your whole body will be full of light. (Matthew 6:22)

There is no doubt that we all agree that the eye is the most important of all the 5 senses. It is the strongest, most powerful form of communication with the outside world. When an individual loses an eye, it becomes a huge problem to them. Jesus gave this sense special attention and you may have noticed this in His miracles. He opened the eyes and healed many blind people. We say, in the Gregorian mass, "You have given sight to the blind".

How can we deal with this sense and what is Christ's message in today's passage?

You notice that Jesus' messages are white or black. For example, He speaks of the good heart and the bad heart. Today, He gives us two kinds of eyes, the simple eye and the evil eye. "Come you blessed of My Father, inherit the kingdom", and in another part, "Depart from Me". Jesus has no shades of grey when He speaks, as we sometimes do nowadays.

Let us talk about what the simple eye is? Is it the naive eye or the eye that does not see anything? Definitely not. The simple eye is not an evil eye, it is an eye full of hope. The person who has a simple eye hopes in everything, is not pessimistic, sees that everything is beautiful, always trusts in God and believes His words. Quite the opposite for the person with an evil eye who does not trust in God; there is a huge wall between them and God.

The simple eye always sees heaven and eternity, these words are not theory. That person looks towards heaven and contemplates on the day they will depart and be with Christ. The simple eye does not involve themselves with other people's business, they look only at their own affairs. Some people look at others, compare themselves with others and are affected if someone else has something they don't have, becoming affected by it. The simple eye thanks God for everything and appreciates the little things.

This is the opposite of the evil eyed person, who gets annoyed, likes nothing, is never happy, not pleased with

> ⁜
>
> THE PERSON WHO HAS A SIMPLE EYE HOPES IN EVERYTHING, IS NOT PESSIMISTIC, SEES THAT EVERYTHING IS BEAUTIFUL, ALWAYS TRUSTS IN GOD AND BELIEVES HIS WORDS.

their life, does not appreciate their friends, are not satisfied with others at church. These people look at the negatives in others, whilst the simple eyed person always concentrates on the good that others have.

If you find yourself looking at others and see good things, then your eye is one of the simple eyes whom Jesus said, "The whole body will be full of light". However, if you always see the shortcomings of others, or tell them all their mistakes, then you are in the category Jesus said is, "An evil eye".

What is the danger of the evil eye?

Let me give you an example: The prophet David had a simple eye. We see this throughout his early life when he was young, a chosen person for his simplicity and his heart. But due to evil it changed his eye; we could not imagine that his life would be affected.

Often, I hear people say, "I can't imagine that I would one day hate someone, or fall into such a sin"; having an eye which changes from simple to evil.

There is another type of eye which the church fathers spoke about and this is the Guide Eye for the body, the internal eye that opens heaven and God. St. John Chrysostom says, if the eye is raised to heaven, then the whole person, with their feelings, their worship and their behaviour sets off to heaven and if the eye is looking down to earth, so it will be captive to the love of self-glory, the hypocrisy of the Pharisees, the richness of the world, the lusts of the body.

They call the eye the controller or the leader. If the leader falls captive then all the soldiers cannot do much, if the ship sinks then what is its benefit if it is filled with treasure? Some people may collect good deeds, prayers, fasting and believe their life is great, but, if their eye is evil, everything becomes darkness. Christ often spoke of the evil eye. For example, the Parable of the Eleventh Hour (The Parable of the Workers in the Vineyard). The workers in the early hours complained that they received the same as those who came at the 11th hour. The landlord replied saying, "I am doing you no wrong... Or is your eye?" (Matthew 20:13,15).

The eye is a big problem, be careful of your eye because if there is darkness or evil so your whole body is darkness, as the Lord Jesus tells us.

How do I know if my eye is simple or evil?

Look at whether you judge others, your look towards them, the feeling in your heart towards them. What direction does your eye look? Does it look towards heaven or earth? Is your eye a simple eye, a lustful eye, a cunning eye, a comparing eye? All these things will determine what sort of eye you have.

How can I acquire a simple eye? Are people born with this simple eye? Definitely not. It is the fruit of the life we live and company with God. It must come from above. It is not a work of human efforts. There are many things in life which the Lord must first touch the heart before there is a change.

Consider the following points:

You need to know which type of eye you have, simple or evil.

Judging yourself is very important so that you know where you stand.

Do not think of your eye as simple when in truth it is an evil eye.

The most powerful thing which enlightens the eye is the word of God. It is true, believe me, where you soak your eye and your heart to be cleansed, like bleach which cleans everything.

Avoid whatever causes you to sin in your life. Don't put yourself in wrong places, which may cause you to sin, so that your eyes don't see things which affect you so you don't judge others or hear things about others which make you sin. Flee from these places, as the Lord said: "If your eye causes you to sin, pluck it out and cast it from you". He didn't mean exactly the word pluck, but to get rid of these things from your life.

Remember to always use The Arrow Prayer (sometimes called The Jesus Prayer), which mentions the name of our Lord Jesus and is effective in protecting our eyes, heart and senses. Repeat this prayer as often as possible, like Bartimaeus did; "Lord Jesus Christ, Son of God, have mercy on me a sinner", until, by the grace of God, He will come and touch your heart.

Chasten your eye. Don't let it roam around, be in control of it and teach your eye chastity.

Always remember, it is not your job to restrain or judge others.

The critical point here is that the Lord comes and touches your eyes. Always say to Him, "My Lord, sanctify my eyes; sanctify everything in me for Your glory and holy name.

Our Good Lord, our Great Lord, as You opened the eyes of the blind, today, we come to You with eyes full of corruption, eyes which have gone far from You, evil eyes. We ask You Lord to lighten my eyes, give us the simple eye, the eyes of babies as You said, "Unless you are converted and become as little children, you will by no means enter the kingdom of heaven". To You is the glory and honour forever and ever. Amen.

Seek First the Kingdom of God

"But seek first the kingdom of God and His righteousness, and all these things shall be added to you" (Matthew 6:30)

Our message today continues our series on the contemplations on the mind of Christ. Notice that this is the longest part of The Sermon on the Mount, which speaks of one topic, but a very important one and deals with a huge problem of our times. It is certainly not Covid, it is far more serious than that, it is 'worry'.

Christ starts by telling us that we cannot serve two masters, God and money. In our faith there is only black or white and nothing in between. Each person has the complete right to choose between the two, but either, or. Christ concludes by saying, "Seek first the kingdom of God".

There are two key points here, the first is 'choice' and the second is 'request'. Since we are still trying to understand the mind of Christ, we must ask ourselves the usual question; what is the aim of these verses? Christ knows well that worry is the biggest enemy of human beings and it has been planted by Satan and he planted this in our hearts.

Dear brothers and sisters, Satan always works contrary to Jesus. Jesus gives light and Satan gives darkness. Jesus gives righteousness and Satan gives sin. Jesus gives peace and Satan gives worry. He always does the opposite of Jesus.

Secondly, Jesus wants to set us free for the final exam. How? When we were young and studying for exams, our families would tell us to just focus on your exams and leave everything else to them. They would tell us that your goal is to pass the exams. So it is with Christ, He tells us not to worry about anything, what we eat, what we drink, what we wear, just focus on and seek the kingdom of God.

> JESUS GIVES PEACE AND SATAN GIVES WORRY.

When I was thinking about worry, I realised that when we were young we never worried. Why? We had a simple view on life, no thoughts on money, treasures, savings, no problems, patient with one another, living with God. Also, all our prayers were accepted and answered, in spite of the simplicity of words and the simplicity of the prayer. But Jesus was so happy with this. Unfortunately, now we use big expressions and big talk but our prayers hardly reach the ceiling of our rooms. We had no enemies. We were straight forward and our yes was yes and our no was no. We lived day by day and Jesus was not a scary God or judge. Absolutely not. He was our soft, gentle, affectionate Father. You know why? Because sin was not a part of our hearts. Worry did not exist in our lives when we were children.

Let's ask ourselves why we need to worry. Sadly, the answer is, we have no trust in God. Our life with Him is weak, we have no faith in Him. Worry is also a product of ambition. When ambition increases it begins to resemble greed. As a consequence, our dreams begin to have too much significance and we put a great deal of hope on achieving these earthly projects. Then, of course, the result is worry. Worry is putting a great deal of confidence in life as if life on this earth is the end. When the balance between life on earth and eternal life becomes swayed, one loses peace because of the huge interest with what exists on earth.

My dear brother and sister, we must agree on one goal; everything on earth must serve the kingdom of God, because eternal life is everything. Yes, everything; your birth, your work, your family, your children, your food, your drink and so on. Everything serves to lead us to the kingdom of God.

Briefly, we see that worry comes because we take on a role which either is not ours or we don't understand. It is not your role to secure, guarantee, protect, and keep safe. No, it is God's role. He said it clearly, that He will definitely do it. For everyone, good or bad, His followers or not, people who accept Him or deny Him.

Hence, our role is to live life as Jesus intended for us. Our role is to live as simple creatures, waiting for the kingdom of God. Christ says that the plants, flowers, birds have no worries. They do not store things up, they live their role just as God created them for. But humans always tend to play different roles.

I have a question, in particular about the recent events; does worry change the outcome of Covid? Does worry change anything or our situation in life? Worrying about exams, money, children, grandchildren or anything else, will never change your situation! On the contrary, it will complicate the situation, as it prevents the hand and the peace of God from penetrating your heart. Thus, we need to submit ourselves.

What should we do to minimise the worry in our lives?

Consider our sins and confess them.

Get enough sleep.

Be realistic. That is, have realistic expectations for certain things which we know will never be achieved by worrying. Things in the past will never be changed, as Jesus said, "Therefore do not worry about tomorrow, for tomorrow will worry about its own things. Sufficient for the day is its own trouble". (Matthew 6:34). Just live for the day.

Sometimes we need a vacation to relax; you need a good friend you can trust to talk with or to talk to a priest.

Jesus is our example; before the Cross He prayed. This is the remedy for worry; deep prayer. Talk to God and leave all in His hands. Pray from the Psalms and read the Bible as you will find many comforting words there, which will give you peace and calmness, such as: "Fear not, for I am with you, I will strengthen you Yes, I will help you, I will uphold you with My righteous right hand (Isaiah 41:10); "Do not fear, little flock, for it is your Father's good pleasure to give you the kingdom" (Luke 12:32); "I will be with you. I will not leave you nor forsake you... Be strong and of good courage; do not be afraid, nor be dismayed, for the Lord your God is with you wherever you go" (Joshua 1:5, 9); "Casting all your care upon Him, for He cares for you" (1 Peter 5:7); "If you can believe, all things are possible to him who believes" (Mark 9:23). Also, in the Paraclete Chapters, Jesus said, "Peace I leave with you, my peace I give to you; not as the world gives do I give to you. Let not your heart be troubled, neither let it be afraid" (John 14: 27). All these verses and many more give us peace and eliminate worry and reveal God's promises to us.

Lord, all we ask and pray to You, our God and heavenly Father, You know our weaknesses, we have no faith, we've lost much time in prayer in our life, but we come toward You today, asking to remove the fear and worry in us, teach us how to trust You, give us peace through Your Holy Spirit, to fo.rtify our life and not to have fear for tomorrow, to have trust in You, also to submit our life completely to Your hands and to learn from the birds and the fish. Teach us also to seek the kingdom of God. Please accept our pray. To You is the glory and honour, forever and ever. Amen.

Judge Not, that You be Not Judged

Matthew Chapter 7 is all about the lives of those who are invited to the Kingdom. So, we find Jesus speaking about this invitation and what our response is.

"Judge not, that you be not judged. For with what judgment you judge, you will be judged; and with the measure you use, it will be measured back to you. And why do you look at the speck in your brother's eye, but do not consider the plank in your own eye? Or how can you say to your brother, 'Let me remove the speck from your eye'; and look, a plank is in your own eye? Hypocrite! First remove the plank from your own eye, and then you will see clearly to remove the speck from your brother's eye" (Matthew 7:1-5).

Today the Lord solves the problem, which is very common to all God's children, which is 'judgement'.

Jesus was sharp in His word "Judge not, that you be not judged", just like, "If you do not forgive, neither will your Father forgive". His language was very sharp. What are Christ's thoughts on this? Why did Jesus, to Him be the glory, forbid judgement? What is the depth of the message of Jesus? Love, reconciliation and forgiveness. Here Jesus wants to say, "It can't be that I bring this deep message of love, calling for forgiveness and reconciliation for all humanity and I forgive you all but you judge one another".

In Christ's eyes, all of us are children of His Kingdom, which means we are all brothers and sisters together, in Jesus. It is not right that a brother judges his brother. They must live in harmony, homogeneity. And this is why Jesus is sharp. Jesus came to cover the sins and weaknesses of all humanity, including you and I, because whoever judges, walks in contrary to Jesus' way. Jesus came to close the gap between us and

Jesus was sharp in His word "Judge not, that you be not judged", just like, "If you do not forgive, neither will your Father forgive".

God and to dissolve the differences between people. We must not segregate and judge each other.

Christ accepts us unconditionally, the seriousness of judgement is not accepting our brothers or sisters, instead of praying for them, we expose them, uncover them before others. Instead we should do what Christ did when He covered the woman caught in adultery.

Why do we judge?

Firstly, it is pride. The person who judges others is arrogant because they are not focusing on their own home or life. Imagine a person whose home is full of rubbish, lust, anger, hypocrisy, impurity, disobedience and breaking of God's commandments. Instead of cleaning their own home they go to the home of their brother or sister and tells them to pick up the pieces of paper that are on the floor. This is exactly what the Lord was talking about? Jesus said, "Hypocrite! First remove the plank from your own eye", clean your house first, and clean the rubbish from your own house before asking your brother or sister to pick up the paper from the floor.

Second, it is not our role to judge, it is God's role. It is not your work or your job to judge others. Who told you to do this? Who gave you consent to do it? Who gave you authority? Let me share a story with you about St. John of Sinai who lived in St. Catherine's monastery. He was a great ascetic and lived a solitary life. His cell was far from everyone. One day another monk went to visit him. St. John asked him about the rest of the fathers in the wilderness and how they were. He replied that all were fine with the blessings of your prayers. He then asked him about a certain monk they all knew was defeated by a certain sin. The father replied, "He has not changed, he is still in his sin". St. John made a huge sigh of disapproval. Suddenly he saw a vision; Christ crucified on the Cross and the angels praising Him. When St. John kneeled to worship Him, Jesus told one of the angels, "Get him away from Me", and He said to St. John, "Do not kneel before Me because you have snatched the judgement from Me". When St. John heard this, he was filled with great fear. The angel took him away and, as he ran away, his robe caught on a hook on the door. He left his robe and ran away naked. Then, St. John of Sinai awoke from the vision and saw the monk still standing beside him. He said to the monk, "Have you been silent for some time? And did you see a vision?" St. John told the monk, "It was a terrible day for me today because I took away the cover which my Lord Jesus protects me with. Christ told me that my robe which became caught on the door was the cover that God protects me from nakedness". Following this, St. John of Sinai, struggled many years in prayer with tears for God to forgive him this sin of judging.

In the Agpeya we pray, "If the righteous one is scarcely saved, where shall I, the sinner appear?" I am struggling to be saved enough, I don't need an extra sin of judging others around me to be added to me.

Mother Teresa said the beautiful words, "If you judge your brother, you have no time to love him, instead of judging him, love him".

Do you know why your brother or sister does what they do? Do you know what their life consists of? What they have been deprived of? Who may have bullied them in their childhood? At school? Who may have upset or annoyed them? Who may have challenged them? What do you know about this person to judge them? What do you know of their circumstances in life? It is not my job or yours to judge.

St. Paul tells us in Romans, "Therefore you are inexcusable, O man, whoever you are who judge, for in whatever you judge another you condemn yourself; for you who judge practice the same things" (Romans 2:1). Christ's goodness, forbearance and longsuffering leads us to repentance. The person who we judge might repent and correct their ways, but may you do not, you may not have time to repent. St. Paul says, "Or do you despise the riches of His goodness, forbearance, and longsuffering, not knowing that the goodness of God leads you to repentance?" (Romans 2:4). There are sins that God despises, judging is one of them.

St. Bachomius said, "Do not despise another person and do not condemn them, even if you see them fall into sin. Because condemnation comes from an arrogant heart, but the humble heart considers all people better than themselves. For what right do you condemn another person? If they fall then the Lord is able to pick them up. If they are good or bad it is not your issue". He also said, "Whoever blames themselves finds mercy before God". He tells us to be like the tax collector who beat on his chest saying, "God, be merciful to me a sinner!" (Luke 18:13) and God accepted his prayer.

St Esnofios said, "If you are humble, God will drive away demons from you, so you should always blame yourself". This sin needs self-control, control of the senses and control of the tongue. At times we may not judge but we are with someone else who judges. What do you do in this situation? Do you keep your mouth shut, remain silent, be passive? If so, perhaps from within you are pleased to sit and listen, especially if that person who is being judged has also annoyed you. The fathers recommend saying, "My friend, sorry, I cannot hear these things about this absent person because I too do the same sins". Doing this has two advantages:

I remind myself of my own sins.

I built the other person who is judging in a good way without hurting them.

When we hear bad things about someone, it may tarnish their image in your eyes, so you can no longer see them in a good light as before, hence you should not hear bad words about another person.

God, gives us the special grace to overcome this in our life, in our church, in our homes. To You is the glory and honour, forever and ever. Amen.

Do not Give what is Holy to the Dogs

"Do not give what is holy to the dogs; nor cast your pearls before swine, lest they trample them under their feet, and turn and tear you in pieces" (Matthew 7:6)

As we continue to understand the mind of Christ, let us meditate together on this difficult verse, which many of us find hard to understand. Jesus often speaks on the purity of the heart as the centre of worship. He also spoke of the simple eye and the dangers of condemning others. In Christ's thoughts, it looks like He wants to caution us from understanding that being simple means being naïve, or lacking wisdom. This is why we see Jesus mixing both simplicity with wisdom, as He said to His disciples, "Therefore be wise as serpents and harmless as doves" (Matthew 10:16). Our Lord urges us to be wise in everything. We will talk of many examples, by the blessings of the Holy Spirit, and see when and how we "give what is holy to the dogs; nor cast your pearls before the swine". The word pearl originates from the Greek word "margritas". The symbol of the pearl in the Bible represents the kingdom of God. Jesus said we must not throw the most precious things to the swine because they will tear them to pieces. Jesus wants to tell us that we should not give the secrets of the kingdom of God or our Bible teaching to anyone who has proved to be useless or inexperienced, or pretending to be religious. We must be cautious and use wisdom. And consider what to give and to whom. In fact, this point is very important, so let's see what the Bible says about this. What are the dogs? What are the pigs? And what is holy?

Dogs in the Bible are a symbol of uncleanliness and defilement. As St. Paul tells us in Philippians, "Beware of dogs, beware of evil workers, beware of the mutilation!" (Philippians 3:2). God likens those who live in evil and sin to dogs and the vomit of dogs who return to their vomit. These types of people never get enough of doing evil, they drink it like water. Also, it is written in Revelation, about the Holy Land Jerusalem, "But outside are dogs and sorcerers and sexually immoral and murderers and idolaters, and whoever loves and practices a lie" (Revelation 22:15). We clearly see that dogs are related to dirt, uncleanliness, evil, sin and bad things. Although the world loves this beautiful animal, we are referring here to the Biblical point of view.

What about the swine or pig? Likewise, pigs are the same, after they clean themselves, they go and roll themselves in the mud and dirt. What do they symbolise in the Bible? They appear as the fake person, who believes that they are following the correct way of Jesus and the teachings of the Bible, but in fact, they make their own rules and their own way of thinking. This, in fact, is a real problem these days. There are many who think that they have the true picture of the Bible, of Jesus and of the correct teachings and they live according to these beliefs, convincing themselves that they are holy, but unfortunately, they are not. We advise them to go back to the Church teachings, and the teachings of the Early Church Fathers, who presented us with the correct picture of our faith and to the Apostles who taught these things over 2000 years ago.

Today, the world has painted a strange picture of the rules of the Bible and the commandments. So, swine, or pigs, are the ones who make their own teaching of what worship is, according to their own desires and think themselves holy, however, from within, they are full of sin, and this is what our Lord Jesus is attacking more than anything.

Solomon said, "As a dog returns to his own vomit, so a fool repeats his folly" (Proverbs 26:11). This resembles a superficial Christian who shows everyone how good and holy they are but from within they are full of dishonesty, deceit, sin, refusing to repent and live with Jesus in purity. Such people, Jesus warns us of, asks us to keep away from and not to follow their counsel.

The Church should not tolerate them, as the Bible says, "Beware of false prophets, who come to you in sheep's clothing, but inwardly they are ravenous wolves" (Matthew 7:15), because their intention is to destroy and divide the Church.

Another application of this verse is, do not share your secrets and your relationship with God as it could be misused, only share it with your confession father. When you do good deeds, they should be done in secret and completely hidden. We should not easily give away the holy secrets to careless people, living in sin and drinking from evil water. It won't work. They should walk in repentance and away from evil. God calls us to have mercy on and love all people, I agree, but we must not leave the door open to heresies.

The final point and the most difficult one, is that we respect the sanctuaries. If the Church respects it, how can the Church put the sanctuaries in the hand of dishonest people? To run the Church? Just as the Priest Eli said to his sons, "You make the Lord's people transgress" (1 Samuel 2:24).

God calls us to have mercy on and love all people, I agree, but we must not leave the door open to heresies.

Throughout the history of the Church, we see in every era, advocates of reform, but unfortunately, they proved to be dishonest and placed the Church in danger. Our Church was established by St. Mark the Apostle and Pope Athanasius. We should not give it to careless, dishonest people, who work for their own benefits and do not care for the benefit of the Church. We should all ask for wisdom, to lead a simple and honest life. Jesus said in the Gospel of St. Luke, "Who then is that faithful and wise steward" (Luke 12:42), to deal with the matters in our lives and also to keep the sanctuaries of our Church precious and valuable as they should be.

I require to have two things:

1. To live faithfully in my inner life and in my application and leadership of anything in life.

2. To be wise so that I do not get into any problems.

Our Good Lord, our Holy God, on this blessed day, we lift our hearts to You. You are the source of all wisdom, give us and the whole Church, in every place, wisdom to deal with any problems that come into the Church. Give us the spirit of discernment and distinction in our lives, not only to be spiritual but to have wisdom. You said Lord, "If any of you lacks wisdom, let him ask of God, who gives to all liberally and without reproach, and it will be given to him" (James 1:5). Please Lord accept and answer our prayers, to You is the glory and honour, forever and ever. Amen.

Ask, and it Will be Given to You

"Ask, and it will be given to you;
seek, and you will find; knock,
and it will be opened to you.
(Matthew 7:7)

As we agreed together, everything in our life serves only one thing, that is, the Kingdom. That is why The Sermon on the Mount is so important in our lives, as believers and children of God. Hence, it is vital for us to understand these chapters very well because they hold the thoughts of Jesus, His desires and plans for us, which is the path that guides us.

In today's passage, Jesus gives us three keys for the kingdom. Often, we take these keys as referring to our earthly needs, but this is not the focus Christ intended. At the end of Chapter 6, Jesus said that the Gentiles seek all these things. He tells us many times not to worry and to seek first the kingdom of God and His righteousness.

Let us familiarise ourselves with these 3 keys, how they work and what they open. When you study the Latin origin of these 3 keys you will find them in the present continuous tense, 'ask', 'seek' and 'knock'. So, Jesus, to whom is all the glory, wants to tell us to use these in our life and in our church. Not only once or twice, but they must be central to all our requests and prayers.

Let us reflect today on how often, in our weekly prayers, we ask for the kingdom? Ok, we are all on pause mode now. When we consider all our requests, we may find that they are all earthly, always walking in the opposite direction to Jesus. He says don't worry, but we worry. He says don't ask for earthly things, but we ask for earthly things. He says don't fear, but we fear. The Lord Jesus said, "I prepare the kingdom for you, it is most important in your life". Ignore the things which keep you busy, eating and drinking, all will come to an end, will finish, we don't know when. The Lord Jesus tells us to busy ourselves with the kingdom. He gives the promise straightaway; 'ask' and straightaway the answer will be given, 'seek' and you find, 'knock' and it will be open to you.

Here we ask, what do You mean seek the kingdom? Does it mean, Lord, move me from earth to heaven? Or, Lord, I want my life to finish? Definitely not! The Lord knows I have a role here on earth and it is an important one, even if it is a simple one, which no one else can do.

> ⁂
>
> THE LORD JESUS TELLS US TO BUSY OURSELVES WITH THE KINGDOM. HE GIVES THE PROMISE STRAIGHTAWAY; 'ASK' AND STRAIGHTAWAY THE ANSWER WILL BE GIVEN, 'SEEK' AND YOU FIND, 'KNOCK' AND IT WILL BE OPEN TO YOU.

Seek the kingdom means prepare me for the kingdom, prepare me for heaven, get me ready, ask, seek and knock; these are the criteria to enter the kingdom. I can't enter the kingdom while I am undisciplined, I am negligent, I am an adulterer and I am a thief. When I pray, I ask, Lord please change me to be a picture fit for entering the kingdom. St Paul said, "But we all, with unveiled face, beholding as in a mirror the glory of the Lord, are being transformed into the same image from glory to glory, just as by the Spirit of the Lord" (2 Corinthians 3:18). Hence, prayer changes and transforms me first, before I ask for anything else.

How am I changed? This is the work of the Holy Spirit in you and I. I need to ask to be filled with God's Spirit, who will convict me, teach me, judge me, who will take from God and give to me. We want to repent from certain things that we do but we can't because the Spirit is not able to work in us due to our heart not being 100% ready, still far away. I am still bodily. When I call the Holy Spirit, He will help me to repent, convict me until I respond, offer my repentance and my confession to the Father, then give the absolution. If we have not had confession for some time, now is the time to do so.

What else do I ask for? Lord let people see You in me, when I talk, my words and my look, to be a salt. The first people to see me are those in my home, my children will see the image of Jesus Christ in me, not a terrifying image. And when I am at church, praying all day, I want it to be the correct picture of Christ? The true picture of mum and dad belongs to Christ, not by words but by deeds, then Christ will be glorified, "Let your light so shine before men, that they may see your good works and glorify your Father in heaven" (Matthew 5:16). I am asking for people to see Your glory everywhere, in my church, in my service, in my home and in my work. May Your glory fill the whole house, my whole life.

The best prayer was what Solomon asked for, after he had finished building the temple, "For the glory of the Lord filled the house of God" (2 Chronicles 5:14). We want likewise, the glory of God to fill the whole world. We say in the Liturgy, "Lead us throughout the way into Your Kingdom, that as in this, so also in all things, Your great and holy name may be glorified, blessed, and exalted in everything honoured and blessed".

In verses 9-11 in this passage, the Lord reassures us by the following example; "Or what man is there among you who, if his son asks for bread, will give him a stone? Or if he asks for a fish, will he give him a serpent? If you then, being evil, know how to give good gifts to your children, how much more will your Father who is in heaven give good things to those who ask Him!" (Matthew 7:9-11). This also tells us, "Your heavenly Father gives the Holy Spirit to those who ask Him!".

It pleases God to give you, pleases Him to fill you, but you don't ask, you don't knock and you don't seek. We complain, asking to eat and drink and be healed, but God tells us to put the most important thing before us, the kingdom.

Our Heavenly, Great Father, who gave us the most precious thing You have, Your Only Son, who was incarnated for our sake, you gave us Your Holy Spirit and raised us to become a temple for the Holy Spirit. You promised us eternal life, you told us, "I am going to prepare a place for you" and when You have prepared it, "I will come and take you and receive you to Myself, that where I am, there you may be also, to see My glory".

On this blessed day, teach us to correct our requests, teach us to correct our direction. Prepare us and equip us for heaven, for the kingdom, so that when the time comes, we will be ready to meet the Bridegroom. Give us the grace to change, give us to be filled with Your Holy Spirit, give us that people see You in us and see Your church and Your children everywhere, filled with glory. To You is the glory and honour, forever and ever. Amen.

Treat Others as You Would have them Treat You

"Therefore, whatever you want men to do to you, do also to them, for this is the Law and the Prophets" (Matthew 7:12)

Today's message is nice and simple, but is full of teachings. Some commentaries say that this verse is related to "Do not judge", and some say it is related to "Ask, and it will be given to you; seek, and you will find; knock, and it will be opened to you". Suddenly, as you can see, after the Lord Jesus finished all His teachings, He placed this verse here and it is called, the golen rule, as you want others to do to you, you also need to do to them.

Other religions, such as Buddhism, have taken this teaching, as has, indeed, the whole world. But what is the truth of this verse? Is it related to judgement, or something else? Remember, our aim is to understand the thoughts of Christ. In reality, this verse summarises all of Christ's teachings on The Sermon on the Mount.

The Lord tells us if you do not want others to lie to you, then you also, do not lie to them. If you do not want others to mock you, then you also, do not mock them. If you want people to respect you, then you respect them. If you want others to not betray you, then you also do not betray. Christ said, "Walk the extra mile and the third; whoever strikes you on one cheek, offer the other one also". Christ asks the person to be heavenly, not limited in their own capabilities. The unlimited things come from the unlimited nature. Think about it for a second, when you have Holy Communion, you are united with Christ, who is unlimited.

Do you not think that Christ can do this inside you? You are the altar of the Holy Spirit who dwells in you. Don't you think that the Holy Spirit is capable of doing things that you can't do it? Therefore, this verse has no limits. No, there is no borders or ceilings to this verse. Then what is it? As you want people to do to you so you, get out of your ego and do to others. You will be raised to the unlimited by the grace and work of the Holy Spirit. In this verse, the Lord raises the ceiling, contrary to what is understood, because in Christianity, we don't give only when we receive. This may be for other religions, because it becomes a moral issue not a spiritual one. Thus, Christ did not come for us to do that, He came with new things, "Behold, I make all things new" (Revelation 21:5).

Today is a call for you and I to get out of the cage. Some of us are afraid of being hurt by others, so they avoid them. Perhaps we have had bad experiences in the past that are keeping us away. We need grace to get out of this prison or this shell. Our call as Christians is not to avoid or distance ourselves from others, but to trade, as in The Parable of the Talents (Matthew 25:14-30). The person who took the one talent and hid it in the ground, Jesus called wicked servant. Hence, our responsibility is not to hide but to trade and make a profit, to win people through our love and sacrifice for them. This represents the personality of our beautiful Lord Jesus, our loving God.

Let's go back to the Golden Rule; treat others as you would have them treat you. When you contemplate on this you will see that there will be no limit to our love and sacrifice for others. However, when we dwell on it we realise the difficulty of applying this in our lives due to our weakness and unworthiness. The only goodness we have is that we are sons and daughters of Christ. We are united with Him, His name is on us, He adopted us and filled us with His Holy Spirit. He has given us the ability to do it if we WANT to, but many people don't want to.

> THE GOLDEN RULE, AS YOU WANT OTHERS TO DO TO YOU, YOU ALSO NEED TO DO TO THEM.

After all the Lord has done for us, He expects us to think and live according to what He has asked from us. But we say, "suppose that they hurt us, despise us, make us sad and so on". I say to you, "blessed are you, because the Lord wants to elevate you to a higher spiritual level". Do not ever think of the price you pay for all these insults. As St. Paul said in Romans, "For I consider that the sufferings of this present time are not worthy to be compared with the glory which shall be revealed in us" (Romans 8:18).

Some people live in this world to take and profit, regardless of the price is. On the other hand, there are those who love and sacrifice all their needs in order to win the soul of others, no matter how hefty may be the loses.

How would you like to live your life? According to your personal thoughts and profits or what the Lord God expects from you, through His grace and the power of the Holy Spirit in you? Imagine if we all, as God's children, came out of our cages and overcome our egos. We would have unconditional and unlimited love and forgiveness to whoever is around us! Our world would definitely be different. This is the call for today's message. In our next sermon, we will outline in detail, the exact path that we should follow to achieve this.

Our Heavenly Father, who has come down to us and given up Your glory and taken our nature. You did the unthinkable and humanly impossible thing in order to grab me by the hand and pull me from hades. I ask you Lord, to give me the characteristics of the new being that resembles Your love and the work of Your Holy Spirit. So, we can offer through You, to all of mankind and the whole world, what you want us to do. To You is the glory and honour, forever and ever. Amen.

Enter by the Narrow Gate

"Enter by the narrow gate; for wide is the gate and broad is the way that leads to destruction,"
(Matthew 7:13)

At the beginning of The Sermon on the Mount, Jesus spoke about the kingdom secretly. Then He gave the commandments for the children, how to pray, today's bread and advises them slowly to raise their eyes from the world in which they are so occupied with and seek God's kingdom and His righteousness. Then Jesus described the children of the kingdom, their behaviour with each other, until He reached the last stage in the sermon where He describes the difficult road which leads to eternal life. He first offered the blessings, then the love, then raised us up slowly to tell us at the end, do not ask for anything other than the kingdom.

Finally, He has planned the road for us. Many become annoyed by the words 'the narrow gate'. What is your personal opinion on this? St. Luke tells us, "Strive to enter through the narrow gate, for many, I say to you, will seek to enter and will not be able" (Luke 13:24). Jesus always gives us two choices. In this world you will find the narrow gate, which is not known to many, whilst the wide gate is well known and many are acquainted with it. I ask again, what is your understanding of the narrow gate? What are Jesus' thoughts on this?

When Jesus loves someone very much, He chooses the narrow gate for them. You tell me how? I tell you to look at Saint Mary; He chose for her a very narrow gate. Didn't He love St. Peter? He gave him a narrow gate too. Have you noticed in the Bible, in the history of the Church, in the Synaxarium or the life of any righteous person, that they went through the narrow gate?

Let us go on a journey to the narrow gate and the wide gate and see who we find in each of these gates?

When Jesus loves someone very much, He chooses the narrow gate for them.

The NARROW gate will have many people suffering, carrying their agony, heavy burdens, walking calmly.

People putting much effort in prayer, fasting, prostrations. These people are filled with the Holy Spirit, virtues, a sweet aroma, focusing on their Bible with reverence, hearing God's voice and submitting their will to Him. You will find people praying in the church and praising, having Holy Communion, living in honesty in every little detail. You will also find people practising repentance for every sin, in order to live in purity. You will find people working continuously in the service, serving others with a spirit of love and God granting them talents. You will find well-known people, mothers, fathers, servants, poor people, sick people carrying their sickness with gratitude, suffering with many tribulations in their lives, with thanksgiving. But these are few.

The WIDE gate is known to many and many will point it out to you. You will find those living a life of lust, worldly desires, breaking the commandments without caring. You will find people filled with pride, boasting at the expense of the church or someone else. Those collecting and accumulating money without being satisfied. People destroying old stores in order to reconstruct bigger ones to store more harvest and to enjoy their future life saying, "Soul, you have many goods laid up for many years; take your ease; eat, drink, and be merry" (Luke 12:19). People forgetting about their poor brothers and sisters, with their desires being mainly for their bodily lusts. People changing God's word, or deviating from it, from the Church Laws in order to make it agree with their own needs. People calling for false liberty, living for today and not worrying about tomorrow. Selfish people, quenching the Holy Spirit, forgetting the voice of the Holy Spirit within them.

People not giving account of their actions and the Bible collecting dust in their homes and no prayer.

Those who take the narrow gate follow in St. Paul's footsteps and say, "In weariness and toil, in sleeplessness often, in hunger and thirst, in fasting often, in cold and nakedness" (2 Corinthians 11:27); or in the footsteps of St. Anthony and many others. The narrow gate truly is narrow. You may find someone caring for a very sick person for the rest of their life, or an elderly person, or an orphan, or perhaps a wife supporting her aggressive husband with contentment, or welcoming a stranger who has no one to look after them, all for Christ.

Jesus places two choices before us, but He never pushes or forces, He just asks, do you want to reach the kingdom? Jesus never changes His word. He said the way that leads to destruction is the very wide road and there are many who take this road. But the way to the kingdom is very narrow and there are few who find it. Often the wide gate dazzles us with lights, many encourage us to take it and some force us to. On the way to the wide gate, you may see signs saying 'come to the narrow gate'. Or some may tell you, 'come out of the wide gate and follow the narrow gate'. In this case, accept the advice from these people and listen to them. This person may be your confession father, or someone who loves you and wants you to leave the wide gate, but you don't take notice of them.

It is not shameful if you are in this wide gate, but it is a shame to continue in it. There are many who have gone through it but got out of it. The good news is that the Lord does not count how long you were on this road. Go and ask those of the eleventh-hour. God gave them the same amount of money as those who came in the early morning. It is His vineyard, He can do what He wants.

Maybe you have been on the wide road and prefer to continue. First, thank God that He has allowed you to live until now. He gives us a chance to change our way. Believe me, you will find many people who make you doubt that Christianity is not narrow. Don't believe them. Believe in God's words. That way has many thieves. St. Augustine says, "Right is right, even if no one is doing it. Wrong is wrong, even if everyone is doing it". Even if you find people that you know, all around you on this wide road, this doesn't mean that you should walk in the same road as them.

Work hard to get into the narrow gate. Don't continue to make the same mistakes. Pray hard. God will support you and give you your heart's desires. No one who desires to live honestly with God, finds God closing the door on them. God responds to the prayer from the soul which desires repentance. Ask from your heart, offer repentance with a true and honest heart. Sit with yourself; first say, thank You Lord for all Your goodness, God gives us many new chances.

Thank You Lord, perhaps in the past I made bad choices, but, with Your long patience, you allowed me to have more time to repent, to choose right, to choose You first before anything and follow You with all my heart. Give me grace, with Your guidance and the work of the Holy Spirit, to choose You. Don't let the devil laugh at me by telling me that the wide gate is the right way, even if all those around me tell me so. I will trust You and Your words. Allow this year to be a blessed and peaceful year all over the world. Thank You Lord for everything. To You is the glory and the honour, forever and ever. Amen.

Wolves in Sheep's Clothing

"Beware of false prophets, who come to you in sheep's clothing, but inwardly they are ravenous wolves. You will know them by their fruits." (Matthew 7:15)

You will also find these words in Luke 6:43-44. Our Lord Jesus begins this passage with the word 'beware' or 'be careful'. He wants to alert us and the Church. When the Christian Church began in the first century and the Holy Spirit came upon believers, many false prophets sprang up. Just as in every crop tares are found, false teachers entered into the midst of the believers. They proclaimed their knowledge, but they were entrapped by Satan, "But there was a certain man called Simon, who previously practiced sorcery in the city and astonished the people of Samaria, claiming that he was someone great, to whom they all gave heed, from the least to the greatest, saying, 'This man is the great power of God.' And they heeded him because he had astonished them with his sorceries for a long time" (Acts 8:9-11). Also, "Now when they had gone through the island to Paphos, they found a certain sorcerer, a false prophet, a Jew whose name was Bar-Jesus, who was with the proconsul, Sergius Paulus, an intelligent man. This man called for Barnabas and Saul and sought to hear the word of God. But Elymas the sorcerer (for so his name is translated) withstood them, seeking to turn the proconsul away from the faith. Then Saul, who also is called Paul, filled with the Holy Spirit, looked intently at him and said, 'O full of all deceit and all fraud, you son of the devil, you enemy of all righteousness, will you not cease perverting the straight ways of the Lord?'" (Acts 13:6-10).

Hence, Christ began to warn and alert the church and the believers against false teachers, who wear sheep's clothing and roam about in the midst of the Church. Also, in Acts 20, the well-known words from St. Paul from Miletus to the Elders, "For I know this, that after my departure savage wolves will come in among you, not sparing the flock" (Acts 20:29). So, there are always dishonest people, hiding in the midst of the Church. Humans are always fascinated by and follow supernatural happenings, which are the result of magic or sorcery and the work of Satan. In the Book of Job, with God's permission, Satan demolished and destroyed all of Job's possessions and his children in no time at all. Fire fell from heaven and consumed all his livestock and servants. God allowed this.

St. Paul tells us, "Let no one deceive you by any means; for that Day will not come unless the falling away comes first, and the man of sin is revealed, the son of perdition" (Thessalonians 2:3). The son of perdition comes at the era of the falling away, "The coming of the lawless one is according to the working of Satan, with all power, signs, and lying wonders, and with all unrighteous deception among those who perish" (2 Thessalonians 2:9-10).

God tells us to be aware. We notice throughout the ages, many liars have appeared, so we must examine and differentiate each person; look at their teachings, their background, and examine the doctrine they are purposing. Consider the story of Charles Russell in 1876, Pennsylvania, USA; he was a member of the Protestant Church until the age of 16 before deviating to the Seventh Day Adventist Church. By the age of 24 he claimed to speak many languages and had many ecclesiastical degrees. He claimed that God spoke to him and he then began the Jehovah's Witness movement, which became a large organisation and still very active in the world today.

Definitely these false teachers spread unacceptable and wrong doctrine. They hide and deny the power of God and oppose the Apostolic teachings of the Church. They come to church in the form of sheep's clothing. There are many movements which entered the Church in order to destroy the Body of Christ. St. John says in his Epistle, "Beloved, do not believe every spirit, but test the spirits, whether they are of God; because many false prophets have gone out into the world" (1 John 4:1).

How do we know these spirits and distinguish them? Jesus said, "Everyone who is of the truth hears My voice." (John 18:37). And He said, "I am the way, the truth, and the life" (John 14:6). Therefore, we must ask for guidance of the Spirit of God, because He is the Spirit of Truth. In order to receive the Spirit of God, we need to:

Be humble so as to be filled with the Holy Spirit and ask for it. The main thing which quenches the Spirit is pride. It is this pride which many of the heretics, who divided the Church, have; a spirit of haughtiness and they refuse to submit. When we are humble, the Holy Spirit fills us and guides us to the truth. When the Spirit of God dwells within the humble person, they escape more and more from people. Insist on asking for perseverance with wisdom, being steadfast in the teachings of the Apostolic Fathers of the Church. Trust in these teachings which were handed to us by the Apostle St. Mark, and do not deviate from them.

Do not depend on your own understanding. Do not rejoice with every new thing that comes out. Ask and learn and be a disciple. St. Paul said to his disciple Timothy, "And the things that you have heard from me among many witnesses, commit these to faithful men who will be able to teach others also"

Be humble so as to be filled with the Holy Spirit and ask for it. The main thing which quenches the Spirit is pride.

(2 Timothy 2:2). He also told him, "That good thing which was committed to you, keep by the Holy Spirit who dwells in us" (2 Timothy 1:14). Therefore, it is very important to preserve the one Spirit that unites us with our holy fathers from whom we received the faith from the saints.

Jesus tells us that we can expose their lies, "You will know them by their fruits" (Matthew 7:16). He also included they won't have hope, they won't change, they do not bear good fruit and they carry bad branches, "And even now the axe is laid to the root of the trees. Therefore, every tree which does not bear good fruit is cut down and thrown into the fire" (Matthew 3:10). Hence, by their fruits you will know them. Here, Jesus gives the Church the authority to besiege the false prophets and judge them based on their teachings and deprive them of ecclesiastical membership and thus, warn the Church against allowing them to enter and not heed their teachings, just as we saw how Simon the Sorcerer was dealt with in Acts.

Christ gives attention to the good trees that bear good fruit and the bad trees that bear bad fruit; a good tree cannot bear bad fruit nor can a bad tree bear good fruit. We will continue this in the next sermon.

To our God is the glory and honour, forever and ever. Amen.

The Trees and Fruits

"Even so, every good tree bears good fruit, but a bad tree bears bad fruit. (Matthew 7:17)

In our previous sermon, we stopped at 'the trees and fruits'. I would like to remind you what Jesus said in Matthew 7 and Luke 3, "Even so, every good tree bears good fruit, but a bad tree bears bad fruit. A good tree cannot bear bad fruit, nor can a bad tree bear good fruit".

Jesus draws our attention to the importance of fruits in our spiritual lives. He also spoke about the Fig tree, which He strongly condemned because it resembled the Pharisees in their worship. They look good from the outside but from the inside they have no spiritual fruits. Let us look at

Christ's beautiful words in John 15, the Parable of the Vine; "I am the true vine, and My Father is the vinedresser. Every branch in Me that does not bear fruit He takes away; and every branch that bears fruit He prunes, that it may bear more fruit" (John 15:1-2).

We also see men of God interested in talking about the fruits. We see the Great St. John the Baptist teaching, "Therefore bear fruits worthy of repentance" (Matthew 3:8). St. Paul the Great often spoke of spiritual fruits in his Epistle to the Galatians and the church fathers spoke of the fruits in our lives. Fruits reflect a successful relationship with God, the fruits are not the aim, however, the fruits are a good indication of the relationship and the level of maturity and stability with God.

How do I know the fruits in my life? I wish that I could have a spiritual mirror to stand before and see how much fruit I have in my life. Unfortunately, this mirror does not exist! Luckily though, you can identify the fruits as follows:

The words of the Bible and Jesus' teachings. Every time you read the Bible you will find Christ speaking of a certain picture or image or shape of the spiritually successful person, the fruitful life of the person who is attached to God and much more. You see it in the people around you. Sometimes you will see the life tree of a person full of repentance, always rebuking themselves, and their live is a

> I WISH THAT I COULD HAVE A SPIRITUAL MIRROR TO STAND BEFORE AND SEE HOW MUCH FRUIT I HAVE IN MY LIFE.

beautiful aroma of repentance. Another person has a life tree full of the enormous fruits of love, from within and from without, love for life, for God, for others. Another person's life tree has the fruits of peace and wherever they go they spread peace and joy. Still another person's life tree is full of heavy fruits that causes its branches to be bent, caused by the humility of the person, and more astonishing, that person is not aware of their tree being full of many fruits. Another has a tree full of fruit for the name of God, they trade for the sake of God, always trading with their talents, working hard with sermons, conferences all over the world and gains for the sake of God. Another person's life tree has good branches of very good and blessed children and a good and successful relationship with God, his house, his work and this is apparent to everyone.

How do I know my fruits? How do I deal with them? There are many things I must do.

I need to know what my talents are, what are the gifts which Christ gave me. I need to know myself, my message in life and what God wants me to do. God never asks the same thing from any two people. Each person has a different message and task according to their talent and gifts which God has given them.

Trade and achieve benefits, for the sake of God. Don't look at yourself, look always for the aim, in order to make a profit, like a very competent trader.

When God gives you fruits, be modest and humble before God and you will see the results. God will surely increase them more and more, giving you more fruits in your life.

Be strongly attached to God, as a branch in the vine, being steadfast in God, "Like a tree planted by the rivers of water, that brings forth its fruit in its season, whose leaf also shall not wither; and whatever he does shall prosper" (Psalm 1:3). This is the secret to a fruitful relationship with God, to be steadfast in Him.

When God gives you fruits (talents), don't touch them, don't crave for them, they are not yours. The moment you look at them, be sure they will be taken away from you. These fruits are for the sake of the glory of God, not for your glory. All these talents which are given to you by God, are not yours.

In the Song of Solomon, we read, "A garden enclosed is my sister, my spouse; a spring shut up, a fountain sealed" (Song of Songs 4:12). This means, when you have fruits in your life, hide them, don't talk about them, don't be proud of them. They are not yours. Keep them a secret, like a garden enclosed, it is between you and God.

Finally, sometimes the fruits may come late in life, as seen in the Parable of the Barren Fig Tree, "A certain man had a fig tree planted in his vineyard, and he came seeking fruit on it and found none. Then he said to the keeper of his vineyard, 'Look, for three years I have come seeking fruit on this fig tree and find none. Cut it down; why does it use up the ground?' But he answered and said to him, 'Sir, let it alone this year also, until I dig around it and fertilize it. And if it bears fruit, well. But if not, after that you can cut it down'" (Luke 13:6-9). Sometimes life, with all its pressures and problems, causes us to not clearly see the right road, coming to know God late in life, delay in understanding the message, during this time there are no fruits. Then the voice of God says, "Cut it down". But the answer will be, "Please Lord, let it alone this year also, I will dig and fertilise around it and will return back to You". We have lost many years without understanding the importance of the essential fruits in your life. Before I thought it was my efforts, my cleverness, my wellness, which would produce the fruit, now I realise that without You I am useless. I can do nothing without You Lord.

God, please give us to be fruitful always in every good work. Make our branches so heavy with fruits for the sake of our King Jesus Christ. God, please give us all the fruits which St. Paul spoke of. To You is the glory and the honour, forever and ever. Amen.

The Path to the Kingdom

"Not everyone who says to Me, 'Lord, Lord,' shall enter the kingdom of heaven, but he who does the will of My Father in heaven" (Matthew 7:21)

Here we meet with Jesus' thoughts at the end of The Sermon on the Mount. Throughout this series we are looking for the mind of Christ; but we have the mind of Christ. The most valuable thing the Church has is found in Chapters 5, 6 and 7 of the Gospel of Matthew.

Jesus presents to us, in this sermon, His thoughts and the works He wants us to follow. He gave us many commandments and invitations to pray, dialogue and requests to receive. Christ gathered all of this for the sake of the kingdom. He spoke of the conditions of entering the kingdom and the gate to enter by. He speaks also, of the parables of the kingdom in Matthew Chapter 13 and, in more detail, in Matthew Chapter 25. We always find Christ pointing to the kingdom.

Sometimes, the path to the kingdom seems difficult and the commandments hard to follow. We often notice, in our modern times, many people making Christianity available to everyone by cancelling out the essential elements of the teachings of Christ. There are two levels here, the level that Christ asks of me and the level I have reached. Some wish to change the level that Christ requested by bringing down the thinking and making it easier. This is wrong because you will not be faithful in what you do. I admit that I am not able to reach or have a long time to get there, but the level set by Christ must be the level we aim for. Jesus' teaching is Black and White, as we mentioned before. He said, either this or that, nothing in between.

Let us talk about this commandment, "Not everyone who says to Me, 'Lord, Lord,' shall enter the kingdom of heaven, but he who does the will of My Father in heaven". Consider the commandment from Deuteronomy, "Beware that you do not forget the Lord your God by not keeping His commandments" (Deuteronomy 8:11). There is always a difference between us and humanity and between us and God on this point, keeping the commandments. In the New Testament, Jesus states this very clearly in the Gospel of St John; He talked about the love of God and keeping His commandments, "If anyone loves Me, he will keep My word; and My Father will love him, and We will come to him and make Our home with him." (John 14:23).

At the beginning of our spiritual life's journey, keeping the commandments does not appear in the forefront. Let us see the stages we go through in our spiritual life.

The first stage is the childhood stage of listening to and hearing stories. We discover God through the stories we hear. At this stage, there is no personal relationship with God, only one of recipient.

Then comes the adolescence stage, in which enthusiasm and praise occurs, where you find yourself with a group and enjoy a life of fellowship with young people like yourself. You want to do many things, you have the fragrance of Jesus, but have no depth with Him.

Then comes the stage of spiritual maturity, in which the person scrutinises everything in their life. Scrutinises their prayers, their actions, their behaviour, their repentance, their service, their dealings with money. This stage opens the door to the beautiful stage, depth or being saturated by God. This is the stage that, by the grace of our Lord, our eyes become open to the commandments and obey the commandments. It comes after many events of our life have taken place, and we have made mistakes and broken many commandments. We begin to have a kind of spiritual awareness, spiritual ground, wisdom and discernment. It is then that I begin to understand what God wants of me. You begin to ask, "God, what do you want me to do?" These words are among the most beautiful words spoken in the Bible. St. Paul, when he was still known as Saul of Tarsus, spoke these words when he fell on his way to Damascus. With his eyes blinded he said, "Lord, what do You want me to do?" (Acts 9:6).

What does it mean to obey the commandments? It means to listen to God's words, to not negotiate them, to keep them as a sword on my neck, to do as the Holy Spirit asks me to do and what the Holy Bible outlines for me and what my confession father directs me to.

As soon as St. Peter the Apostle heard the Lord's words, "Launch out into the deep and let down your nets for a catch" (Luke 5:4), after he had been toiling all night and caught nothing, he spoke the words, "Nevertheless at Your word I will let down the net" (Luke 5:5). As a result, the nets were filled to nearly breaking, due to the great number of fish caught, because he listened to His words and obeyed the commandment.

Obedience to the commandments indicates great wisdom, as we read in Proverbs, "The wise in heart will receive commands" (Proverbs 10:8). The Lord said to the rich young man, keep the commandments. When the Lord sent the disciples for preaching, in Matthew 28, His last words in this chapter were, "Teaching them to observe all things that I have commanded you; and lo, I am with you always, even to the end of the age." (Matthew 28:20). This is the message of the Church, it is a trumpet call throughout the ages and times, in which every servant and teacher stands, memorise what I have commanded you, repeating the words of Christ.

The Lord gave us many commandments and told us to learn the old and the new, "Unless your righteousness exceeds the righteousness of the scribes and Pharisees, you will by no means enter the kingdom of heaven" (Matthew 5:20). Christ also tells us, "A new commandment I give to you, that you love one another; as I have loved you, that you also love one another" (John 13:34) and also asked us to keep away from the love of money and the lustful eye. Christ also asked us to, "Love the Lord your God with all your heart, with all your soul, with all your strength, and with all your mind, and your neighbour as yourself" (Luke 10:27). The important point to understand here is that our Lord wants us to keep all the commandments, without exception. You can't pick and choose, some to live your life with and others to ignore. Christ tells us, "Whoever therefore breaks one of the least of these commandments, and teaches men so, shall be called least in the kingdom of heaven; but whoever does and teaches them, he shall be called great in the kingdom of heaven" (Matthew 5:19).

> OUR LORD WANTS US TO KEEP ALL THE COMMANDMENTS, WITHOUT EXCEPTION. YOU CAN'T PICK AND CHOOSE, SOME TO LIVE YOUR LIFE WITH AND OTHERS TO IGNORE.

The application of the commandments is very important. St. John Chrysostom said, "If you keep a few commandments, then you will be small or miss out, and if you are lacking in them, you are small in the general resurrection". St. Basil the Great said, "What is the use of a fortress if it is fortified on every side but has a small door on its edge, through which enemies can infiltrate and enter and then harass or kill the people within". The two saints stress that the fortress must be complete. All doors must be closed and every opening must be blocked, to prevent the little foxes from entering the heart; once they are in they begin to eat and eat and become larger and eventually you won't be able to get them out.

Let us ask a question: "Is the commandment easy or hard?"

From Jesus' point of view, the commandment is difficult. It is like a yoke or a burden; but He describes this yoke as easy and light, "Come to Me, all you who labour and are heavy laden, and I will give you rest. Take My yoke upon you and learn from Me, for I am gentle and lowly in heart, and you will find rest for your souls. For My yoke is easy and My burden is light" (Matthew 11:28-30). The commandment is difficult because, to keep it, you need to struggle and work hard, but each commandment is followed by joy and gives you hope. They are a great gift from God, especially at the beginning of a person's spiritual path as they fight their lusts.

There is no doubt that some commandments are difficult, "If anyone desires to come after Me, let him deny himself, and take up his cross, and follow Me" (Matthew 16:24); "If anyone wants to sue you and take away your tunic, let him have your cloak also" (Matthew 5:40); "And whoever compels you to go one mile, go with him two" (Matthew 5:41); "But I say to you, love your enemies, bless those who curse you, do good to those who hate you, and pray for those who spitefully use you and persecute you" (Matthew 5:44); "Do not lay up for yourselves treasures on earth, where moth and rust destroy and where thieves break in and steal; but lay up for yourselves treasures in heaven, where neither moth nor rust destroys and where thieves do not break in and steal" (Matthew 6:19-20); "And do not fear those who kill the body but cannot kill the soul. But rather fear Him who is able to destroy both soul and body in hell" (Matthew 10:28); "And if your right hand causes you to sin, cut it off and cast it from you; for it is more profitable for you that one of your members perish, than for your whole body to be cast into hell" (Matthew 5:30). All these are very hard and difficult, we may be filled with fear from them, we say, "Don't introduce this difficult Christianity to us". Does this mean that they are not Jesus' teachings? Definitely not! Otherwise He wouldn't say them.

But all the fathers, all the commentaries, all who experience our Lord Jesus, the fathers in the wilderness, the early church fathers, the wisdom of our confession fathers, all agree that the difficulty gradually fades away and turns into sweetness. When a person is led by the Bible every day and turns the commandments into action, the bitterness is overcome by joy. This means the more a person perseveres in reading the Bible daily and being saturated with the thoughts of Christ, they are immersed in it and saturated by His words. Bit by bit the mind will change, then the Lord brings something very beautiful, which is called GRACE. The work of grace works in you and supports you and encourages you and makes the road easier for you and pleases you.

The commandment becomes easy when a person carries the yoke and thinks of the good that will come after the commandment is fulfilled. The commandment is difficult for a proud person, but the person who practises humility and meekness, will find the yoke easy, "Take My yoke upon you and learn from Me, for I am gentle and lowly in heart, and you will find rest for your souls" (Matthew 11:29). Hence, the humble person finds the commandment easy to apply. It becomes easy when you believe in it and take it in your mind. This is the picture God wants for me, then we ask, "What Lord, do you want me to do?" and you do it. The commandment becomes easy when we know it is healing to our soul. We will feel God's love and feel that we are near Him, we will feel His bosom, we will rejoice and place everything else under our feet.

St. Simon the Theologian said, "He who keeps the commandments, the commandments preserve him, love him, protects him and frees him from passions and sins". The fathers suggest to start with ONE commandment; keep it, obey it and it will lead you to follow another commandment. Hence, forgiving someone gives you peace, you love them more, this humbles you more, which then helps you to repent and begin to know yourself more. In contrast, breaking one commandment causes you to break another and so on.

Christ Himself obeyed the commandments, "For I have not spoken on My own authority; but the Father who sent Me gave Me a command, what I should say and what I should speak" (John 12:49). He humbled Himself and became obedient to the Cross. St. Paul tells us in his Epistle to the Philippians, "Let this mind be in you which was also in Christ Jesus, who, being in the form of God, did not consider it robbery to be equal with God, but made Himself of no reputation, taking the form of a bondservant, and coming in the likeness of men. And being found in appearance as a man, He humbled Himself and became obedient to the point of death, even the death of the cross" (Philippians 2:5-8).

Hence, obedience to the commandments is critical.

May God open our eyes and our hearts on this day, to understand this dimension of the mind of Christ and go into the depths and spiritual fulfilment, in obedience to the commandment and the grace of our Lord supports us all. To You is the glory and honour, forever and ever. Amen.

Do not Lose Your Way

"...And then I will declare to them, 'I never knew you; depart from Me, you who practice lawlessness!'" (Matthew 7:22)

These words can be quite hard and quite scary. I wonder how these words can proceed from Christ's mouth, who is so kind and tender to us all. However, here He says, "I never knew you; depart from Me, you who practice lawlessness!". May the Lord help us to reveal the mind of Christ in these words.

In Pope Shenouda's well known poem, The Release of the Spirit, he wants to say, that while God is kind and loving and gives many opportunities for us to repent and is patient with us all, nevertheless, has a whip in His hand. He says these words in this passage, to every person, especially those who serve Him (the servants).

God gathers all those who He rejects, according to His view; there are many, even servants who delivered sermons, visited the desolate, collected money for the poor, but did not live a righteous life and their lives were full of cheating, lying and hypocrisy. There are servants who do their service in order to acquire authority, for their own glory. They involve themselves in many social activities, but deep down, in their hearts, you will not find mercy, forgiveness, acts of love or sacrifice. You will find virtual words, recited words, which have the appearance of the power of the Spirit, but are empty from within. They do not have grace or power. They use Biblical verses very skilfully, in a very powerful way and say their prayers on time, but there is no love or mercy in their hearts and do not work according to God's will. Therefore, Christ cried out and said, "I never knew you; depart from Me, you who practice lawlessness!" (Matthew 7:23).

You stood before Me, just to take from Me the authority, the power and the grace to preach in My name, you did not stand before Me in Spirit, and you did not open your Bible. You were not serving Me, you were serving something else. I did not know you, neither did you know Me. If you did know Me, you would have known what I wanted of you, you would have known My thoughts and kept My commandments. Truly, poor is the person whom the Lord says these words to. In the past we did not often see these kinds of servants, but now these categories of people do exist. Their lives have no mercy, work of love or sacrifice. Their lives from the inside are decadent. Their lives are without remorse and with hardened hearts that do not have the fear of God. Therefore, God will say to them, "I do not know you".

Thus, a servant may live the life of deception, but in the end, the Lord God may say to them, "I do not know you". God forbid, may no one hear these words. Christ left these words till the end of His Sermon on the Mount, after He spoke of love, mercy and blessings. Then He revealed to us His justice; especially where many people are deceived in this world. May God not allow us to be counted among those who live the life of deception. I try to always be positive in my talks, but this time I cannot be. Today the Lord says to every servant, including me; do not lose your way, concentrate on your service and its aim.

Sometimes we lose our way through the system in which we serve. The Lord asks, "Keep your eyes on Me, keep your ears listening to My voice"; "My sheep hear My voice, and I know them, and they follow Me" (John 10:27). "Keep your eyes on your inner soul and your repentance. Your salvation is your first priority, then

> Today the Lord says to every servant, including me; do not lose your way, concentrate on your service and its aim.

all other services come next. Live according to My will and commandments, be as righteous and repentant as possible. Feed on My words, stand in front of Me and pray earnestly". That is what the Lord wants from us, to be filled with the Holy Spirit, so we can take power, grace, strength and help; "I will lift up my eyes to the hills, from whence comes my help? My help comes from the Lord" (Psalm 121:1-2). That is my role, but unfortunately this translates to a chain of many activities and stories which are far from standing before God. I fear the days will come and we stand in front of Him and He will say, "Go away from Me I do not know you".

We ask you Lord, that You guide, teach, connect us to Your way, so we can hear Your voice, let our eyes remain focused upon You and give us the grace to serve You according to Your will. Hence, we can serve with love, understanding, wisdom and to please You, through Your grace. Above all, please Lord, accept our humble service as You accepted from the little boy with the 5 loaves and 2 fish. To You is the glory and honour, forever and ever. Amen.

www.ingramcontent.com/pod-product-compliance
Lightning Source LLC
Chambersburg PA
CBHW020157090426
42734CB00008B/846

HERITAGE BOOKS
AN IMPRINT OF HERITAGE BOOKS, INC.

Books, CDs, and more—Worldwide

For our listing of thousands of titles see our website
at
www.HeritageBooks.com

Cover photo courtesy of Edward S. Gregory, III

Published 2007 by
HERITAGE BOOKS, INC.
Publishing Division
65 East Main Street
Westminster, Maryland 21157-5026

Copyright © 2003 Barbara Venton Montgomery, Ph.D.

Other books by the author:
Lovinia's Child: A Depression Tale
Women Short-Changed by History

All rights reserved. No part of this book may be reproduced or transmitted in any form or by any means, electronic or mechanical, including photocopying, recording or by any information storage and retrieval system without written permission from the author, except for the inclusion of brief quotations in a review.

International Standard Book Number: 978-0-7884-3355-5

I0176124

Wonderful “Wicked” Women of the World

Barbara Venton Montgomery, Ph.D.

HERITAGE BOOKS
2007